**NEW, REVISED, COMPLETELY UPDATED
SECOND EDITION**

**STILL THE ONLY INVESTMENT GUIDE
YOU'LL EVER NEED**

★ A National Best-seller
★ A Book-of-the-Month Club Special Alternate
★ A Fortune Book Club Main Selection

"Tobias's cool, spare, readable style lays bare the rapacious scams of the Wall Street moneymen, and . . . provides a conservative strategy to protect hard-earned savings."

—*New York* Magazine

"Absolutely delightful . . . Sound advice on how to deal with the whole investment process. Don't let its light touch fool you—it's got more than its share of wisdom."

—*Stock Market Magazine*

"There comes a point in the reading of any financial guide when the mind collapses. This usually happens around the point when the book starts asking if you've thought of option straddles . . . Andrew Tobias, in his witty and succinct [book], has a pretty sound explanation for these sinking spells . . . It's all a matter of organizing your priorities. And the most basic priority is that before you can start making money through financial investment, you have to figure out how to stop losing money through simple squandering. What Tobias has to say is as rational as a pocket calculator."

—*The New York Times*

"A good primer for anyone who doesn't want to die poor."

—*Washington Star*

ALL YOU NEED TO KNOW ABOUT BANKS by Robert Wool
and John A. Cook

THE BUSINESS WRITING HANDBOOK by William C. Paxson

EVERYBODY'S INVESTMENT BOOK: HOW TO INVEST
UP TO $5,000 EVEN IF YOU DON'T HAVE IT by Edward
Malca and Sandra Choron

GUERRILLA TACTICS IN THE JOB MARKET by Tom
Jackson

HIGH FINANCE ON A LOW BUDGET by Mark Skousen

HOW TO BUY STOCKS by Louis Engel with Peter Wyckoff

HOW TO WAKE UP THE FINANCIAL GENIUS INSIDE
YOU by Mark O. Haroldsen

MARKETING YOURSELF: THE CATALYST WOMEN'S
GUIDE TO SUCCESSFUL RESUMES AND INTERVIEWS
by The Catalyst Staff

MOLLOY'S LIVE FOR SUCCESS by John T. Molloy

NO-NONSENSE MANAGEMENT by Richard S. Sloma

184 BUSINESSES ANYONE CAN START AND MAKE A
LOT OF MONEY by Chase Revel

168 MORE BUSINESSES ANYONE CAN START by Chase
Revel

THE ONLY INVESTMENT GUIDE YOU'LL EVER NEED by
Andrew Tobias

SPEAK FOR SUCCESS by Eugene Erlich and Gene R. Hawes

WEALTH & POVERTY by George Gilder

WILLIAM DONOGHUE'S COMPLETE MONEY MARKET
GUIDE by William E. Donoghue

YOU CAN NEGOTIATE ANYTHING by Herb Cohen

Andrew Tobias

The Only Investment Guide You'll Ever Need

BANTAM BOOKS
TORONTO · NEW YORK · LONDON · SYDNEY · AUCKLAND

THE ONLY INVESTMENT GUIDE YOU'LL EVER NEED

A Bantam Book / published by arrangement with
Harcourt Brace Jovanovich, Inc.

PRINTING HISTORY

Harcourt Brace edition published February 1978
6 printings through September 1978

Book-of-the-Month Club edition published February 1978

Bantam edition / February 1979

2nd printing . . . . August 1980
3rd printing . . . . . . December 1981
Bantam revised edition / July 1983
6 printings through May 1986

ISBN 0-553-23563-X

Published simultaneously in the United States and Canada

PRINTED IN THE UNITED STATES OF AMERICA

KR   15   14   13   12   11   10   9   8   7

Contents

To my broker—even if he has,
from time to time, made me just that.

This book is tax-deductible.

Acknowledgments

I would like particularly to thank Sheldon Zalaznick and Clay Felker, the editors with whom I worked most closely for more than four years at *New York* magazine. And also: *New York* magazine for permission to borrow from material I first published there; Carol Hill, whose patience and enthusiasm border on the divine; John and Rochelle Kraus, Laura Sloate, Murph and Nancy Levin, Ken Smilen, Martin Zweig, Burton Malkiel, Alan Abelson, Yale Hirsch, Paul Marshall, Robert Glauber, Stuart Becker, Marie Brenner, Jesse Kornbluth, Don Trivette, Gabriel Perry, and Peter Vanderwicken; *Fortune, Business Week, Forbes,* the *Wall Street Journal,* and the *New York Times;* and Texas Instruments, without whose pocket calculator I would be a broken man.

Although much of what I know I have learned from these people and institutions, whatever egregious faults you—or they—may find with this book are strictly my own.

A.T.

STILL THE ONLY INVESTMENT GUIDE YOU'LL EVER NEED?

If it is brassy to title a book *The Only Investment Guide You'll Ever Need*, it's downright brazen to revise it. Yet not to do so would have been worse, partly because so much has changed since this book first appeared, and partly because so many people, against all reason, continue to buy it. (Nearly a million to date.)

Some things don't change. Individual Retirement Accounts and Keogh Plans are still among the few truly good things in the financial world. A penny saved, if you're in any sort of tax bracket, is still as good as two pennies earned. It still makes sense to buy low and sell high, as it always has and always will (and as many people, lacking perspective, never do). It still makes sense to minimize transaction costs if you invest in stocks with any frequency; and to avoid the market altogether if you haven't the resources or temperament to deal with it.

But chapter 4 has been completely revised to reflect the new and more favorable ground rules for IRAs and Keogh Plans, as well as the new Salary Reduction Plan. Also added: a legal way to cut taxes on a short-term gain to practically nothing. (I don't think it should be legal, but as long as it is, you may as well know about it.) Chapter 3 takes into account such new creatures as high-interest checking accounts and zero-coupon bonds (which happen to be a fine way to fund an IRA or Keogh Plan). Also, thoughts on why preferred stocks may have a place in your life after all. And a never-before-revealed account of my first day at the races (beginner's luck). Chapter 2 has been updated and should save the average household hundreds of dollars a year. The chapters on the stock market have been improved. The chapter on inheriting $1 million has been revised to accommodate the problem of inheriting $2 million. All the appendices have been updated, even to the point of replacing a dated "Cocktail Party Financial Quip to Help You Feel Smug" with a newer one (to help you feel even smugger).

And more.

So one investment decision that must be addressed right away: When much of what follows is unchanged, *should readers of the 1977 edition impoverish themselves to the extent required to purchase its successor?* Yes, please! We have purposely brought it out in paperback rather than hardcover to keep the lead time short and the cover price low.

Part One

Minimal Risk

CHAPTER 1

If I'm So Smart, How Come This Book Won't Make You Rich?

You have to watch out for the railroad analyst who can tell you the number of ties between New York and Chicago, but not when to sell Penn Central.
—Nicholas Thorndike

Here you are, having just purchased a fat little investment guide we'll call *Dollars and Sense,* as so many investment guides are (although the one I have in mind had a different title), and you are skimming through idea after idea, growing increasingly excited by all the exclamation marks, looking for an investment you would feel comfortable with. You page through antique cars, raw land, mutual funds, flower bonds, Krugerrands—and you come upon the section on savings banks. Mexican savings banks.

The book explains how by converting your dollars to pesos you can earn 12% on your savings in Mexico instead of 5 to 8% here. At 12%, after twenty years, $1,000 will grow not to a paltry $2,917, as it would at 5½%, but to nearly $10,000! What's more, the book explains, U.S. savings banks report interest payments to the Internal Revenue Service. Mexican banks guarantee not to. Wink.

The book does warn that if the peso were devalued relative to the dollar, your nest egg—whatever it had grown to by then—would shrink proportionately. But, the author reassures, the peso is one of the stablest currencies in the world, having been pegged at a fixed rate to the dollar for 21 years; and the Mexican government has repeatedly stated its intention not to devalue.

Now, how the hell are you, who needed to buy a book

2

to tell you about this in the first place, supposed to evaluate the stability of the Mexican peso? You can only assume that the author would not have devoted two pages to the opportunity if he thought it were a poor risk to take—and *he's* an expert. (Anyone who writes a book, I'm pleased to report, is, ipso facto, an expert.) And, as a matter of fact, you do remember reading somewhere that Mexico has *oil*—pretty good collateral to back any nation's currency. Anyway, what would be so dreadful if, as your savings were doubling and tripling south of the border, the peso *were* devalued 5 or 10%? That would be nothing compared to what happened to you last time round in the stock market.

So, frustrated by inflation and impressed by the author's credentials, you take *el plunge*.

And for 18 months you are getting all the girls. Because while others are pointing lamely to the free clock-radios they got with their new 5½% savings accounts, you are talking Mexican pesos at 12%.

Comes September 1, 1976, and Mexico announces that its peso is no longer fixed at the rate of 12.5 to the dollar, but will, instead, be allowed to "float." Overnight, it floats 25% lower, and in a matter of days it is down 40%. Whammo. Reports the *New York Times:* "Devaluation is expected to produce serious immediate difficulties, most conspicuously in heavy losses for Americans who have for years been investing dollars in high-interest peso notes." How much is involved? Oh, just $6 or $8 *billion.*

You are devastated. But you were not born yesterday. At least you will not be so foolish as to join the panic to withdraw your funds. You may have "bought at the top" —but you'll be damned if you'll sell at the bottom. The peso could recover somewhat. Even if it doesn't, what's lost is lost. There's no point taking your diminished capital out of an account that pays 12% so you can get 5½% in the United States.

And sure enough, in less than two weeks, on September 12, 1976, the float is ended, and the Mexican government informally repegs the peso to the dollar. (Only now one peso is worth a nickel, where two weeks ago it was worth eight cents.) You may not know much about international finance (who does?), but you know enough to sense that, like a major housecleaning, this 40% devaluation in Mexico's currency ought to hold it for a long, long time. In fact, you tell friends, for your own peace of mind you're just as glad they did it all at once rather than nibbling you to death.

And then on October 26 the peso is floated again, and slips from a nickel to less than four cents. Since Labor Day, you're down 52%.

Aren't you glad you bought that book?

(Everything changes and nothing changes. In 1982 the peso was devalued again. This time by 80%.)

This immodestly titled book—the title was the publisher's idea, in a weak moment I went along—is for people who have gotten burned getting rich quick before. It is the only investment guide you will ever need *not* because it will make you rich beyond any further need for money, which it won't, but because *most* investment guides you *don't* need.

The ones that hold out the promise of riches are frauds. The ones that deal with strategies in commodities or options or gold are too narrow. They tell you *how* you might play a particular game, but not whether to be playing the game at all. The ones that are encyclopedic, with a chapter on everything, leave you pretty much where you were to begin with—trying to choose from a myriad of competing alternatives.

I hasten to add that, while this may be the only investment guide you will ever need, it is by no means the only investment guide that's any good. But, sadly, reading three good investment guides instead of one will surely not triple, and probably not even improve, your investment results.

The odd thing about investing—the frustrating thing—is that it is not like cooking or playing chess or much of

anything else. The more cookbooks you read and pot
roasts you prepare, the better the cook—within limits—
you are likely to become. The more chess books you read
and gambits you learn, the more opponents—within limits—
you are likely to be able to outwit. But when it comes to
investing: trying hard, learning strategies, knowing a lot,
becoming intrigued—all these ordinarily admirable attri-
butes may be of little help, or actually work against you. It
has been amply demonstrated, as I will document further
on, that a monkey with a handful of darts will do about as
well at choosing stocks as most highly paid professional
money managers. Show me a monkey that can make a
decent veal parmesan.

If a monkey can invest as well as a professional, or nearly
so, it stands to reason that you can, too. It further stands to
reason that, unless you get a kick out of it, you needn't
spend a great deal of time reading investment guides,
especially long ones. Indeed, the chief virtue of this one
(although I hope not) may be its brevity. This one is about
the forest, not the trees. Because if you can find the right
forest—the right overall investment outlook—you shouldn't
have to worry much about the trees. Accordingly, this
book will summarily dismiss investment fields that some
people spend lifetimes wandering around in. For example:
It is a fact that 90% or more of the people who play the
commodities game get burned. I submit that you have now
read all you need ever read of the following not-cheap
books: *The Fastest Game in Town*, *Trading Commodity
Futures* (Reinach); *Getting Rich in Commodites, Currencies,
or Coins—Before or During the Next Depression* (Vichas);
Sensible Speculating in Commodities (Angrist); *Guide to
Commodity Price Forecasting* (Jiler); *Point and Figure
Commodity Trading Techniques* (Zieg); *The Commodity
Futures Game* (Terweles); and *Computer-Proven Commod-
ity Spreads* (Angell).

This thing about the forest and the trees—about one's
degree of perspective—bears further comment, particularly
as for many of us it is second nature to feel guilty if we

"take the easy way out" of a given situation. If, for example, we read the flyleaf and first and last chapters of a book, to get its thrust, instead of every plodding word.

I raise this not only because it could save you many hundreds of hours stewing over investments that will do just as well unstewed, but also because it leads into the story of The Greatest Moment of My Life.

The Greatest Moment of My Life occurred in the Decision Analysis class at Harvard Business School. Harvard Business School uses the "case method" to impart its wisdom, which, on a practical level, means preparing three or four cases a night for the following day's classroom analysis. Typically, each case sets forth an enormous garbage dump of data, from which each student is supposed to determine how the hero or heroine of the case—inevitably an embattled division manager or company president—should ideally act. Typically, too, I could not bring myself to prepare the cases very thoroughly.

The format of the classroom discussion was that 75 of us would be seated in a semicircle with name cards in front of us, like United Nations delegates, and the professor would select without warning whomever he thought he could most thoroughly embarrass to take the first five or ten minutes of class, solo, to present his or her analysis of the case. Then everyone else could chime in for the remainder of the hour.

On one such occasion, we had been asked to prepare a case for Decision Analysis, the nub of which was: What price should the XYZ Company set for its sprockets? Not coincidentally, we had also been presented with a textbook chapter containing some elaborate arithmetic/alegbraic way of determining such things. The theory behind it was simple enough—charge the price that will make you the most money—but the actual calculations, had one been of a mind to do them, were extremely time-consuming. (This was just before pocket calculators reached the market.)

The professor, a delightful but devious man, noting the conspicuous absence of densely covered yellow notepaper by my station, had the out-and-out malevolence to call on me to lead off the discussion. I should note that this occurred early in the term, before much ice had been broken and while everyone was taking life *very* seriously.

My instinct was to say, with contrition: "I'm sorry, sir, I'm not prepared"—a considerable indignity—but in a rare moment of inspiration I decided to concoct a bluff, however lame. (And here is where we get, at last, to the forest and the trees.) Said I: "Well, sir, this case obviously was meant to get us to work through the elaborate formula we were given to determine pricing, but I didn't do any of that. The case said that XYZ Company was in a very competitive industry, so I figured it couldn't charge any *more* for its sprockets than everyone else, if it wanted to sell any; and the case also said the company had all the business it could handle—so I figured there would be no point in charging *less* than everyone else, either. So I figured they should just keep charging what everybody else was charging, and I didn't do any calculations."

The professor blew his stack—but not for the reason I had expected. It seems that the whole idea of this case was to have us go round and round for 55 minutes beating each other over the head with our calculations, and *then* have the professor show us why the calculations were, in this case, irrelevant. Instead, class was dismissed 12 minutes after it began—to thunderous applause, I might add—there being nothing left to discuss.*

Now let me return to commodities.

My broker has, from time to time, tried to interest me in commodities. He trades commodities for many of his clients and—almost as proof of his faith in the product—for his own account as well. He has direct access to the head commodities man at his firm, a major New York brokerage house. He tells of clients who have churned $5,000 into $500,000.

---

*Herewith a list of all my other successes at Harvard Business School: I graduated.

"John," I ask, "be honest. Do *you* make money in commodities?"

"Sometimes," he says.

"Of course, *sometimes,*" I say, "but overall do you make money?"

"I'm making money now. I'm up $3,200 on May [pork] bellies."

"But overall, John, if you take all the money you've made, minus your losses, commissions, and taxes, and if you divide that by the number of hours you've spent working on it and worrying about it—what have you been earning an hour?"

My broker is no fool. "I'm not going to answer that," ne sort of gurgles.

It turns out that my broker has made around $5,000 before taxes in four years of commodities trading. Without a $10,000 profit once in cotton and a $5,600 profit in soybeans he would have been massacred, he says—but of course that's the whole idea in this game: a lot of little losses but a few enormous gains. He can't count the number of hours he's spent working on and worrying about commodities. He went home short sugar one Friday afternoon after it had closed up-limit (meaning that he was betting it would go down, but instead it went up so fast he didn't have time to cover his bet, and now he stood to lose even more than he had wagered), and spent the entire weekend, and his wife's entire weekend, worrying about it. So maybe this very smart broker, with his very smart advisors, and their very smart computer readouts, has made $2 or $3 an hour, before taxes, for his effort. And he wants *me* to play? He wants *you* to play?

If 90% of the people who speculate in commodities lose (and 98% may be a more accurate figure), the question, clearly, is how to be among the 10% (or 2%) who win. If it is not just a matter of luck, then it stands to reason that the players who have the best chance are insiders at the huge firms—Hershey, Cargill, Iowa Beef, etc.—who have people all over the world reporting to them by Telex on the slightest change in the weather, and who have a minute-to-minute feel for the market (whether it be the market for frozen orange juice, cocoa, wheat, or what-have-you). These players have, too, the backing and nerve to resist getting whipsawed out of the market when it moves against them. You are not such an insider, but those who are would be delighted to have you sit down at the table and play with them.

If, on the other hand, it *is* just luck, then you have just as good a chance as anybody else for the jackpot, and all you're doing is gambling, pure and simple, hoping to be lucky, and paying commission after commission to a broker who, friend or brother-in-law though he may be, cannot bring himself to give you the right advice. He'll give you advice on October broilers, on the frost in Florida, on the technician's report he claims somehow to have seen before anybody else. Gladly. What he won't tell you—or it will cost him dearly if he does—is that you shouldn't be in the game at all.

Class dismissed.

Similarly: antique cars, wine, autographs, stamps, coins, diamonds, art. For two reasons. First, in each case you are competing against experts. If you happen already to be an expert, then you don't need, and won't pay any attention to, my advice anyway. Second, what most people fail to point out as they talk of the marvelously steady appreciation of such investments is that, while what you would have to *pay* for a given lithograph doubtless rises smartly every year (or used to, anyway), it's not so easy for the amateur to turn around and *sell* it. Galleries usually take a third to a half of the retail price as their cut—so a print that cost $100 and appreciated in five years to $200, retail, might bring you all of $100 when you went back to the gallery to sell it. Meanwhile, neither print nor wine nor diamonds nor Rolls would have been paying you dividends (other than psychic); indeed, *you* would have been paying to insure them.

I gave a speech to this effect in Australia, in 1981, just

as the first faint flaws were beginning to appear in what was then a very hot diamond market. *Nothing* is forever, I suggested, not even the 15% annual appreciation of diamonds. When I finished, a mustachioed gentleman with a bushy head of previously owned hair came up to say how much he agreed with my remarks. "Diamonds!" he scoffed (you could see the disgust in his face); "you couldn't be more right." And for a minute there I thought I had met a kindred spirit. *"Opals,"* he said. *"That's* where the money is." The fellow, it developed, sold opals.

As a child, I collected first-day covers (specially post-marked envelopes). Sure enough, every year they cost me more and more. Recently, discovering them in the back of a closet after a hiatus of nearly twenty years, I called a local collector I had reason to know was on the acquisition trail. (I saw his notice on the supermarket bulletin board.) Knowing you always do better if you cut out the middleman, I figured on selling them to him direct. These are beautiful first-day covers we are talking about, from the forties and fifties—hundreds of them. They had cost anywhere from 25 cents on up (although, in those days, so had a week in the country).

"How much does your collection weigh?" the buff asked, once I had suitably whetted his interest.

"How much does it *weigh*?" I asked. "Is your collection on a diet? It weighs a few pounds, I guess."

"I'll give you $25 for it," he said. Checking around, I found this was not an unfair price. I'm going to wait another twenty years and try again then.

Commemorative medallions (and so forth) issued ad nauseam as "instant collectors' items" by the Franklin Mint served to make the original shareholders of the Franklin Mint rich, but are much less likely to do the same for you. Their silver, gold, or platinum content is only a fraction of the selling price.

Gold itself pays no interest and costs money to insure. It is a hedge against inflation, all right, and a handy way to buy passage to Leichtenstein, or wherever it is we're all supposed to flee to when the much ballyhooed collapse finally materializes, but if you're looking for an inflation hedge you might do better with silver, of which more further on.

Broadway shows are fun to invest in, but you have to *pay* for your opening night seats (at least if you invest as little as I do, you do); and even if the show you back gets rave reviews, you are likely to lose all or part of what you put in. A show can linger on Broadway for a year or more, with packed houses on weekends, and not return its backers a dime.

Chain letters never work.

Things that look like cosmetics companies but are really chain letters in disguise, like Glenn Turner's Koscot Interplanetary and Holiday Magic—where the big money to be made was not in selling cosmetics, but in selling franchises to sell franchises to sell franchises (to sell cosmetics) —don't work either.

Things that involve a personal salesman who is full of enthusiasm at the prospect of making *you* rich don't work. The richer he hopes to make you, the faster you should run.

There are, in fact, very few ways to get rich quick. Fewer still that are legal. Here's one: Take $5,000 (borrow it if you have to), place it on number 22 at the nearest roulette table, and win $175,000. Don't laugh. Many complicated schemes, if they were stripped of their trappings and somehow reduced to their underlying odds, would be not much less risky. It's the trappings—the story, the pitch—that obscures the odds and persuades people to ante up the $5,000 they'd never dream of betting at roulette.

Anyway, enough of the things that won't do you much good, and on to some things that might.

CHAPTER 2

A Penny Saved Is Two Pennies Earned

A taxpayer is someone who doesn't have to take a civil service examination to work for the government.
—*Stock Trader's Almanac*

You are in a higher tax bracket than you think. At least, most people are. And this number—your tax bracket—is critical to understanding your finances.

If you earn $11,000 and pay $1,100 in federal income tax, that does *not* mean you are in the 10% tax bracket. (Any more than if you earn $110,000 and pay $11,000.) On *average* you are paying 10% of your income in federal tax, but that's not what's important. What's important in making financial decisions is how much tax you pay on the *margin*—on the last few dollars that you earn.

Because the income tax is graduated, you pay no tax on the first few dollars you earn, but a lot on the last few. That may average out to 10%; but, in the case above, if you earned another $1,000, approximately *26%* of it would go straight to the government (about $190 in federal income tax, another $70 or so in Social Security), and *that's* your tax bracket. Unless you happen to be subject to local income taxes as well. In New York City—admittedly the most brutal example possible—yet another $95 would go to state and city income taxes, so that you, the $11,000-a-year subway-riding secretary, would be in the 35.5% tax bracket. Congratulations.

When you add in sales taxes and property taxes, of course, the bite is even worse. But such taxes, which are not directly tied to what you earn, don't count in figuring your tax bracket.

Second example:

If you are single and, after all deductions and exemptions, report a taxable income of $42,000 (or if you are married and jointly report $60,000), you pay $450 of the next $1,000 you earn in federal tax. Conversely, if you gave an extra $1,000 to charity—or lost it in the stock market—you could at the same time lower your tax bill by $450, and so really be out only $550. This is what's meant by being in the 45% tax bracket.

If you live in California and report this kind of income, welcome to the 51% tax bracket. In New York City, 55%. The table on page 14 will give you an idea of your own tax bracket.

(Social Security tax, although included in the first example above, does not actually figure into investment decisions. Investment income does not increase the tax; deductions, like capital losses or interest expense, do not lower it. So from here on, even though you have to pay it, we can and will ignore the Social Security tax.)

To figure your bracket more accurately, just haul out last year's federal and local tax returns and calculate how much more tax you would have had to pay if you had earned an extra $1,000. Don't forget that the additional local taxes you incur would count as a deduction in figuring the federal tax—assuming that you itemize your deductions. In the second example, New York State and City taxes came to $183 on the incremental $1,000, so the amount of extra federal tax was calculated not on the full $1,000, but on the remaining $817.

The other way to figure it is to see how much in taxes you would have *saved* if you had earned $1,000 *less*. This way your tax bracket may come out a few percentage points lower, because the less you earn, the lower your tax bracket. It doesn't make a lot of difference, but technically you would do it the first way if you wanted to know how much of some additional income—say, dividends—you would get to keep after taxes; and you would do it the second way if you wanted to know how much you would save in taxes by taking an extra deduction, such as a loss on a stock.

The idea is not to come up with some precise number, or to refigure your taxes every time the Red Cross asks for $5, but simply to have a reasonably accurate feel for where you stand.

Let us assume for the rest of this chapter that you are in the 50% bracket, or not far from it. Do you know what that means?

YOUR APPROXIMATE TAX BRACKET

| SINGLE | | MARRIED *(Filing Jointly)* | |
Taxable Income Above:	Is Taxed At:	Taxable Income Above:	Is Taxed At:
$ 2,300*	11%	$ 3,400*	11%
$ 3,400	13%	$ 5,500	13%
$ 4,400	15%	$ 7,600	15%
$ 8,500	17%	$ 11,900	17%
$10,800	19%	$ 16,000	19%
$12,900	21%	$ 20,200	23%
$15,000	24%	$ 24,600	26%
$18,200	28%	$ 29,900	30%
$23,500	32%	$ 35,200	35%
$28,800	36%	$ 45,800	40%
$34,100	40%	$ 60,000	44%
$41,500	45%	$ 85,600	48%
$55,300	50%	$109,400	50%

*No tax on income below $2,300 (single) or $3,400 (joint).

IMPORTANT NOTES:

1. These figures are for 1983. There may be further jiggering in the tax rates; but barring a drastic change, you shouldn't be off by more than a point or two using this table in 1983, 1984, or 1985.

2. Social Security tax does not figure into most financial decisions and so is not included above. If it were, it would add about 7% to each of the brackets (or nearly 10% if you

It means that if your boss gave you a $1,000 bonus or raise, you would get to keep $500.

It means that "time-and-a-half for overtime," since it is all earned on the margin, is not such a posh deal after all. After taxes, it may be no more valuable to you—or even less so—than any other "time."

It means that 5½% interest in a savings account nets you less than 3% (while inflation, which is *not* tax-deductible, may eat away purchasing power at a much faster rate).

---

are self-employed) on earned income up to a current ceiling—sure to go higher—of $35,700.

3. Don't forget to add state and city income taxes. But don't forget, either, that under current law, local taxes are deductible in figuring your federal tax. So if you're in the 50% federal tax bracket and the 11% California bracket, the combined result is not 61% but 55.5%. Half your California tax will, in effect, be made up by the deduction you get to take.

Florida, Texas, Washington, Nevada, and Wyoming currently have no income tax. In Alaska, they pay *you*! Here are the top income tax brackets in the rest of the country:

AL: 5% on income over $6,000. AZ: 8% over $6,000. AR: 7% over $25,000. CA: 11% over $25,000/$50,000 (single/joint). CO: 8% over $13,352. CT: up to 9% on investment income only. DE: 13.5% over $50,000. DC: 11% over $25,000. GA: 6% over $10,000. HI: 11% over $61,000. ID: 7.5% over $5,000. IL: 2.5%. IN: 1.9%. IA: 13% over $76,725. KS: 9% over $25,000. KY: 6% over $8,000. LA: 6% over $50,000. ME: 10% over $25,000. MD: 5% over $3,000. MASS: flat 10% on investment income. MI: 4.6%. MN: 16% over $35,915. MS: 4% over $5,000. MO: 6% over $9,000. MT: 12.1% over $38,400. NE: up to 8.5%. NH: 5% on dividends and interest. NJ: 3.5% over $50,000. NM: 2% over $100,000. NY: 14% over $23,000. NYC: 18.3% over $23,000. NC: 7% over $10,000. ND: 4% over $30,000. OH: 5.6% over $100,000. OK: 6% over $15,000. OR: 10.8% over $5,000. PA: 2.2%. RI: up to 11%. SC: 7% over $10,000. TN: 6% on dividends and intrest. UT: 7.75% over $7,500. VT up to 12%. VA: 5.75% over $12,000. WV: 9.6% over $200,000. WI: 10% over $48,200.

It means that an 8% tax-free bond is worth as much to you as a 16% taxable one.

It means that the first $100 of dividends you receive (or $200 if you file a joint return), being tax-exempt, is worth twice as much to you as $100 ($200) of interest. (So even if you've sworn off the market, you should find some solid common or preferred stock to hold forever just to generate that much in dividends.)

It means that a $1,000 long-term capital gain can be worth $300 more to you than a $1,000 short-term gain. And that taking a loss while it is still short-term can save more than twice as much in taxes as taking a long-term loss.

It means, above all, that a penny saved—not spent—is *two* pennies earned.

Consider: If you were planning to eat out tomorrow night, as you do every Thursday night, for around $30 with the tip, but you ate at home instead for $5, you saved $25. You have $25 more in the bank than you otherwise would have had. To *earn* an extra $25 for your bank account, you would actually have to earn $50: half for you, half for the tax men.

So if you want to pile up a little nest egg, or a big one, the first thing you might consider—even though you've doubtless considered it before—is spending less rather than earning more. Which is what this chapter's about. If you're in the 50% tax bracket, it's twice as effective—and often easier.

If you purchased a car that averaged 30 miles to the gallon instead of 15 . . . and if an average gallon of gas over the next few years costs a buck twenty . . . then after having driven 50,000 miles you would have saved $2,000, cash, on gas alone, which, in the 50% tax bracket, would be like having *earned* $4,000.

What's more, the cars that get the best gas mileage often cost the least. This despite the fact that in terms of the most important feature by far—getting you where you're going—they are identical to the higher-priced models. By buying an "economy car" you save substantially on the purchase price; substantially on your insurance bill (the less expensive the car, the lower the theft and collision premiums); substantially on gas; substantially on maintenance; and substantially on interest (if you finance the purchase). In all, the financial decision to be "automotively frugal"—while it is a decision you have every right not to make—could mean as much to you as having an extra $30,000 or $40,000 working for you in a savings account.

Charles Revson, the late cosmetics tycoon, ordered his Cepacol by the case. By so doing, although it was the furthest thing from his mind, he did better investment-wise than he ever did in the stock market. In the stock market, with his Revlon-made fortune, Revson perennially blew tens of thousands of dollars on one or another speculation. But on Cepacol he was making 10, maybe 20 or even 30% a year, after tax.

He made it two ways: the discount he got for buying the super-economy size, in bulk; and the discount he got, in effect, by beating inflation. He got a year's worth, or two, at last year's price. If he had kept the money he spent on Cepacol in a savings account at 5½%—for him, 2½% after tax—and taken it out bit by bit to buy Cepacol in the one-at-a-time 59-cent size, where would he have been? This way, he saved maybe 30%, tax-free.

The lesson is clear, even if you are one of those people with naturally pleasant breath.

Buying a case of wine at a 10% discount ties up, say, $45 . . . but you earn $5 tax-free by doing so ($5 off the normal $50 price). If that's just three months' worth of wine for your family, over the course of the year you will save $20 by keeping $45 tied up—an annual return of 44%! Tax-free.

The point is not to save $5 on a case of wine, but to do as much of your buying this way as is practical. In the aggregate, it might tie up an extra $1,000. But between beating inflation by buying now and buying in bulk when items are on sale (or getting a by-the-case discount), you could easily be earning 20, or even 40%, on that $1,000—tax-free. That's $200 to $400 a year the average family can come out ahead—*with no sacrifice whatever*. It's not enough to make you rich, but neither is $1,000 in a savings bank.

This is the chicken-hearted way to play commodities, guaranteed safe for all but compulsive eaters. Forget pork bellies on 10% margin and all those other near-surefire ways to get fried. I am "long," as of this writing, a case of Campbell's soup, fourteen boxes of private-label tissue paper, four giant-sized tubes of Ultra-Brite toothpaste (bought at distress prices), several kegs of Heinz catsup, and much more. I was "short" sugar during the 1975 insanity, which is to say I wouldn't buy any. I just ate down my inventory. Wholesale sugar prices subsequently fell from 64 cents back down to 9 cents and I went "long" a few pounds.

Where to put this mountainous investment? Besides the obvious, like a pantry or basement, if you have such spacious luxuries, you might also consider building your hoard under a bed or table, with a bedspread or tablecloth over the top. I know this is absurd, but I'll bet you can fit thirty cases of economy-sized tuna under just one table. Or make it a bench and put a board over it, with a cushion. Water jugs, bouillon cubes, a can opener (don't forget that!)—plan your portfolio, which doubles as a disaster hoard, and buy it on sale, in bulk. (If you're hoarding tuna, you've obviously got to hoard mayonnaise, too.)

This idea of a disaster hoard, by the way, is not such a foolish one. Nor is it "gloom and doom." Disasters *do* occur—floods, earthquakes, power outages, blizzards, civil disorder . . . and it does make sense for every household to accumulate—now, when there's no need to, at sale prices—enough nonperishables to last a while. A gallon of peanut butter. A case of tuna. A case of canned fruit. Several gallons of water and juices. Such a modest stockpiling protects not just individuals, but serves the social interest as well. Just as the nation is stronger if there are strategic stockpiles, so is the social fabric a little less susceptible to disruption or panic if everyone has an added layer of security. Odd words, I know, in tranquil times— but harmless ones, at worst.

Don't tell me about botulism, either—out of 1.03 trillion cans of food sold between 1926 and 1982, only six produced fatal cases of botulism. Canned food lasts years. In any case, if you rotate your cases of food and drink, the way you used to rotate the sheets on your bed in camp— top to bottom, bottom to laundry, fresh one on top—you'll never let anything get too far out of date.

If this sort of investment takes up storage space, it also takes less effort: fewer trips to the store. And you are much less likely to run out of things. I don't think there was a day in Charles Revson's life that his breath did not smell medicine-fresh.

Now here are a few more conventional ways to save money:

● Fly now, pay now. The best way to earn 18 or 20% on your money, risk-free, is by not going into hock to a department store or bank credit card. That's what most of them charge. Particularly if you do not itemize your deductions, and so cannot get Uncle Sam to bear some of that interest expense, it is folly to pay such rates if you can possibly avoid it. Yet many people keep money in a savings account, earning 5½%—which might be only 4% after taxes—at the same time as they are paying 20% to buy on time. They are earning 4 cents on each dollar with their left hand while paying out 20 cents with their right. That's a loss of 16 cents a year on every dollar—or, if theirs is a family perpetually a couple of thousand dollars in hock, $320 a year, year after year. Wasted.

Before investing $2,000 in some biotechnology stock your dentist's pushing—and believe me, I have any number of impoverished friends who do just that—pay off your credit cards and "earn" 20% risk-free, tax-free each year.

Because not having to pay 20% (say) is as good as *earning* 20%.

Even if you do itemize your deductions—and you probably do—the only way it makes sense to borrow at 20% is if you have some risk-free way to earn *21%*. It's as simple as that.

(To someone in the 50% tax bracket, borrowing at 20% is really like borrowing at only 10%; but so, naturally, is *earning* 20% really like *earning* only 10%.)

Granted, there is something to be said for disciplining yourself not to touch your savings—that money is sacred, a last resort, and so on—and it's hard to put a dollar value on that discipline. But 20%?

● Similarly, if less dramatically (because the rates are lower), you can "earn" upwards of 10%, completely risk-free, by not financing your car. Again, this is particularly compelling if you do not itemize your deductions and hence cannot lay off part of the finance charge on the government. Why pay 13% on a $6,000 loan when you have $6,000, or at least a good chunk of it, sitting in savings accounts or a money-market fund earning 8 or 10% *taxable* interest?

(Nonetheless, when you go to buy a car, ask enough questions about financing—what the monthly payments would work out to, etc.—so that the salesman assumes you will. Financing, every bit as much as air-conditioning or a vinyl sunroof, is a high-margin option for the dealer, and he may be able to find an extra $50 or $100 for you in the deal he makes. Only when the deal is firm and he is committed to the price should you pull out your checkbook. He's got his negotiating ploys; why shouldn't you have yours?)

● "Ah," you are thinking. "Surely he is not now going to tell me I should pay off my mortgage." And I am not (although if it was taken out at 16%, and 11% mortgages are available as you read this, why, then, surely it has crossed your mind to refinance). The difference between a house and a car, or a vacation paid for on time, is that a car depreciates, a vacation disappears altogether, but a house, with any luck, *ap*preciates. It may not be the sure thing it once was; and there are times when mortgage rates are so high it plainly makes more sense to rent. But there is a big difference between borrowing to buy something that appreciates and borrowing something you merely consume. Indeed, the most valuable asset many families own is a big fat 8% mortgage, taken out years ago. If your signature adorns such a document, for heaven's sake don't pay it off any faster than necessary!

● When buying auto or homeowner's insurance, shop around for the best price, and "self-insure" by taking as much of the risk yourself as you can comfortably afford. You do this by choosing the highest possible "deductible" category. In the case of auto collision insurance, this usually means paying the first $250 or $500 of damage yourself, instead of $50. Unless you are a dreadfully unskilled or unlucky motorist, your savings in premiums will more than cover the extra money you might have to pay out in accidents. This is especially true because even people who are fully insured hesitate to hit their insurance companies for small claims, knowing that if they do their rates may go up or their policies be canceled when they come up for renewal. Why pay for coverage you may not even use?

Sometimes the saving on a high deductible is so slight you may as well take the fuller coverage, but this is not often the case. As a general rule, the higher your premium, the greater the incentive to choose a high deductible.

Allstate not long ago was charging an adult driver in Columbus, Ohio, $208 for collision and comprehensive coverage on a 1981 Chevy Citation with $100 deductible. The same driver who chose a $500 deductible exposed himself to—at most—$400 more risk per accident, but cut his annual premium by $94. The odds were probably with him to take the higher deductible, but not nearly so much as if he had happened to own, say, an '81 Scirocco. There the rate fell from $336 to $184—a $152 annual saving. And had he owned an '81 Corvette, he would have saved $246 a year by choosing the $500 deductible.

Homeowners' insurance on a $500,000 frame house in West Hollywood recently was offered by one large company at $2,803 a year if you took the $100 deductible; $2,503 a year with a $250 deductible; $2,228 a year with a $500 deductible; and $1,802 a year with a $1,000 deductible. (Unfortunately, as is frequently the case, no higher deductibles were offered.) Where is the madman who would pay an extra $1,001 a year ($2,803 versus $1,802) to get an extra $900 of coverage ($100 versus $1,000 deductible)?

One last reason to take high deductibles: you will save yourself the hassle and aggravation of making claims.

And a caution: It used to be that Uncle Sam automatically shouldered a portion of any uninsured loss. Casualty losses above $100 were tax deductible. Now that's only true to the extent such losses exceed 10% of a taxpayer's adjusted gross income.

● If you live in California and have a clean driving record, call 20th Century Insurance for a quote: (213) 704-3000, collect. If you qualify for coverage, you are likely to cut your auto insurance bill by a third or more.

● When buying life insurance, *shop around*. Says an FTC spokesman, "Cost variations of over 100% for essentially identical coverage are not uncommon."

There are two basic kinds of life insurance: "term" and "whole" (which is also called "straight" or "ordinary"). With term insurance all you pay for—and get—is protection. If you die, they pay. With whole life you are buying a tax-sheltered savings plan as well. Your policy accumulates "cash values," also known as "living benefits."

Term insurance rates start very low but go up every year. Whole life rates start high but remain constant.

Insurance salesmen are very eager to sell whole life policies because their commissions on these are so much higher than on term policies. (And that, in turn, is because the insurance company profits are higher.) *Don't buy!* You would be wiser to buy renewable term insurance and do your saving separately. (With a renewable policy you are assured of continuing coverage even if your health deteriorates.)

The problems with whole life:

1. Many policies pay low interest.

2. It is impossible for a nonexpert to tell a good policy from a bad one.

3. There is a tremendous penalty for dropping the policy, as many people do, after just a few years.

4. When insurance is needed most, you can get five or six times as much protection for your money with term as with whole life. A 35-year-old who pays $200 for $100,000 of term insurance would pay $1,200 to $1,400 for a like amount of whole life.

In later years, and particularly beyond the age of 50 or 55, term insurance premiums rise rapidly. But by then you may have a less urgent need for life insurance. The kids may be grown, the mortgage paid off, the pension benefits vested. You will still need to build substantial assets for retirement, and to protect your spouse; but there are better ways to save for old age than whole life.

Don't squander what you save buying term insurance instead of whole life; just invest it at a higher rate of interest.

The most economical insurance policies are generally the group policies arranged by an employer or association. Beyond that, the first place to look for small amounts of insurance is the local savings bank or savings-and-loan. In Massachusetts, New York, and Connecticut there is Savings Bank Life Insurance. In Massachusetts, particularly, it is a terrific deal. There's also a new policy, Savers Life,

FOR $100,000 OF RENEWABLE TERM INSURANCE

A Healthy:	Shouldn't Pay Much More Than:
20-year-old	$ 160 a year
25	160
30	175
35	200
40	250
45	350
50	500
55	800
60	1,300
65	2,200
70	3,500

These rates are for men. Women should pay about the same rates as men five years their junior.

that's being sold by S&L's throughout much of the country. If all you need or can afford is $25,000 or $50,000 of term insurance, this is a good buy. A $25,000 Savers Life policy, renewable to age 70, costs a 30-year-old $4.40 a month (slightly less for a woman). After five years the rate jumps—for the next five years—to $5.16 a month. That's all of $62 a year. It then jumps (age 40–44) to $91 a year; to $137 (45–49); to $214 (50–54); to $330 (55–59); to $520 (60–64); and, in the final five years, to a still not too dizzying $826 a year. To find out who in your area offers Savers Life, if anyone, call 800 223-7608 (in New York: 212 753-6531) or write American International Life, 70 Pine St., New York, NY 10005.

Another convenient and often economical way to buy small amounts of term insurance is through the offers constantly being mailed to bank credit-card holders.

But about life insurance remember this: bulk purchases are rewarded by better rates. Four $25,000 policies will cost you a lot more than one $100,000 policy, and three $100,000 policies will cost you a good deal more than one $300,000 policy. Among the many insurers who in 1983 were offering low rates on $100,000 and up of term insurance: ITT Life (Minneapolis), Bankers National Life (Parsippany, NJ), First Colony Life (Lynchburg, VA), Old

Line Life (Milwaukee), American Agency Life (Atlanta), and Fidelity Union Life (Dallas).

For an analysis of how much life insurance you should carry, see the appendix "How Much Life Insurance Do You Need?"

● If you already have a whole life policy purchased in the days when interest rates were low, and if it is of the type that pays no dividends—cash it in (having first obtained substitute coverage elsewhere).

If your whole life policy does pay dividends, and you are allowed to borrow against it at 5 to 8% interest, it's OK to keep it—assuming you *need* life insurance (not everyone does). But be sure to borrow every penny of cash value if you can invest the proceeds elsewhere, safely, at a higher after-tax rate. (Or use what you borrow at 6% to pay off your 14 and 18% loans!) You need never repay a policy loan. It is simply deducted from the proceeds of your policy when you die.

Throughout much of 1981 and 1982, many people were able to take cash values borrowed at 6% and lock up 14% interest on long-term Treasury bonds. Just by doing some paperwork, they came out $800 a year ahead (before taxes) on every $10,000 so borrowed.

● Skip overpriced insurance you *don't* need, including: life insurance for children; credit life insurance (offered as an option when you take out a loan)—a good buy only for the very old or terminally ill; flight insurance; mail-order accident insurance; car rental insurance; any health or accident insurance sold door to door.

● For more on insurance—how to collect if your spouse is the victim of a fantasy sex hanging gone awry, and that sort of thing—I suggest another pricey paperback, *The Invisible Bankers: Everything the Insurance Industry Never Wanted You to Know*. This recommendation is shameless, because I reap 18 cents for every copy sold; but the insurance industry has too long operated without benefit of public scrutiny.

● A solar water heater that costs $1,000 to install but saves $200 a year on your utility bill is like an investment that returns 20% tax-free.

● Simple insulation may be the best "investment" you can make, returning as much as 35% or more, tax-free, in annual savings on heating and cooling. Why put $1,500 into the stock of some utility and earn $150 in annual taxable dividends if you can put the same money into insulation and save $150 tax-free on your utility bill? (Check also the federal and state tax credits that may be available to encourage such energy-saving investment.)

● Own your phones. For as little as $14.95, once, you can save up to $40 a year in rentals.

● SPRINT, among others, is a big money-saver on long-distance calls after five, or if you travel, or if you have kids away at school. Trivial? Just having two kids use SPRINT for their weekly calls, instead of phoning home collect, can easily save $700 during four years of college.

● A lot of people find each year that they have almost enough deductions to make itemizing worthwhile—but not quite. If you fit this category, or if you have barely enough deductions to itemize and thus save very little by doing so, consider bunching your deductions into every second year. Plan to itemize in 1984 and 1986, for example, but to take the standard deduction in 1983 and 1985. *Don't* make the year-end charitable gifts you normally would in 1983—make them in January 1984. (Likewise, local tax payments, medical payments, and any other potential deductions you may be able to push into 1984.) Come December 1984, *do* make your charitable contributions, prepay local taxes and so forth. In half the years, you'll have the same standard deduction you would have had anyway. But in the other half you might find yourself with an extra $1,000 or $2,000 in deductions. That's a savings of $300 to $600 every second year, if you're in the 30% tax bracket, just from knowing when to write out your checks.

● Write away for the Best Products, Sears, and Spiegel catalogs and keep them on your reference shelf. (Best Products, Box 26527, Richmond, VA 23261—name brands at hefty discounts and fast service—a one-time $1 charge to be put on their mailing list; Sears, Sears Tower, Chicago, IL 60684; Spiegel, Box 8282, Philadelphia, PA 19170.) When you need to buy something, check the catalogs first. If nothing else, this will give you a better idea of the kind of bargain you are getting (or not getting) down the street.

● Avoid buying lottery tickets with your spare dollar at the checkout counter. The state lotteries pay out barely 50 cents in prizes for every dollar they take in; but since all the big prizes are heavily taxed, the odds are even worse. Heads you win 30 cents, tails you lose $1.

● Discount gas, most experts agree, is just as good as advertised gas.

● You will use appreciably less of it if you have radial tires and if you drive smoothly. Rapid accelerations are murder on gas mileage; unnecessary braking is a means of converting kinetic energy, through friction, to useless heat. "Good driving habits" and a well-tuned engine can save as much as a third of a family's gasoline bill.

● Quit smoking. There's $300 or $400 a year right there, plus a big savings on your life insurance . . . although by adding five or ten years to your probable life span you will greatly increase the cost of your retirement. On second thought, smoke all you want.

● Have your doctor write prescriptions for generic, not brand-name drugs. The only difference is the price—often a difference of 200 or 300%.

● Private-label merchandise is often made on exactly the same production line, with the same ingredients, as the more expensive advertised brands. Aspirin is aspirin, no matter how elaborate the commercials get.* Bleach is bleach. It is a sad fact of American consumer patterns that

---

Consumer Reports is devastating in comparing such brands as Bayer, Bufferin, Anacin, and Excedrin with plain 59¢-a-jar private-label aspirin. The difference is almost entirely in price, with here and there some caffeine or a trace of antacid or an aspirinlike analgesic thrown in.

poor people, in particular, avoid private-label brands, despite the potential savings, so persuasive is national advertising. For example, private-label shaving cream, menthol or plain, is occasionally on sale at 59 cents. Believe me, it works just as well as the name brands on the next shelf that sell for $1.59.

Granted, not all private-label merchandise is as good as its name-brand competition. None of it, presumably, is better. But is it really worth 80% more to you to sneeze into a genuine Kleenex-brand "kleenex"?

You *can* get by on $165,000 a year

Many of us spend a great deal of time worrying about our money; few of us use that time to make a sensible plan. Where am I? Where do I want to be? How do I get there? This means, simply, making a rough list of everything of significance you own and another of everything you owe. Subtract what you owe from what you own and you have your net worth. The general idea is to have this number be positive.

Better still, to have it grow a little each year.

(It's also helpful to calculate your net worth exclusive of things you would find it awkward to do without, like your house.)

If you make up such a personal balance sheet once a year—tax time is as good as any—you will begin to get an idea which way things are headed.

The other exercise, of course, is to make up a rough statement of profit and loss: income minus expenditures. Where does all that money *go*? Could you budget things so as to save a good chunk of money each year?

Most of us feel we couldn't get by on a penny less. But all a family struggling to get by on $190,000 a year need do is look down the street to see a family that—somehow—manages to get by on $165,000 a year. (They do their own pool maintenance.) The family struggling on $24,000 need only look down the street to see one surviving—don't ask me how—on $18,500. And that family need just . . .

The point is that you *can* save money, if you're willing to make some sacrifices. And it's wise to do so. Because even forgetting retirement needs, "rainy days" and all that, if you can only arrange things to come out a little ahead each year, instead of a little behind, you will quickly find your financial security and, not long afterwards, your standard of living improving. Money does make money. The rich do get richer. And they sleep better.

Saving is difficult, but less so when you have a goal and a plan. To sacrifice any given night on the town makes little sense. What's another $60? But as part of a plan to pay off all consumer loans within the year, say, or to build a net worth of $25,000 in five, a sacrifice that would otherwise seem pointless—and depressing—can be purposeful indeed. Satisfying, even.

No one wants to pass up something because he can't afford it. But to pass it up because he *wants* to—because his eye is on a higher goal—is quite a different thing.

Having said all that (none of it original), let me suggest an obvious way to save: The day your paycheck comes, put 10% of it, automatically, without question, into a separate savings vehicle. It can be a savings account or a mutual fund or an IRA or some combination of accounts—but do it. (Your employer may be able to do it for you, which is ideal, because the best way to avoid temptation is never to see the cash in the first place.) Simply live as if you were making $15,000 instead of $16,500; $36,000 instead of $40,000; $90,000 instead of $100,000.

Alternatively, at the same time you pay your rent each month, or your mortgage, make another "must" payment, without fail: to your savings.

These are ancient notions, but helpful. As with any regimen, the hardest part is getting into the habit. As your pile mounts, it becomes much easier.

YOU SAY YOU HAVE NO ASSETS?

Saving this much annually by shopping, driving, phoning, financing, etc., more efficiently . . .

If you are in this tax bracket:	$500	$1,000	$1,500	$2,000	$2,500
		. . . is as good as having this much earning 8% taxable interest for you in a savings account:			
20%	$ 7,812	$15,625	$23,438	$31,250	$39,063
30%	8,929	17,857	26,786	35,714	44,643
40%	10,417	20,834	31,250	41,667	52,083
50%	12,500	25,000	37,500	50,000	62,500

CHAPTER 3

The Case for Cowardice

This broker calls his customer for four straight years and each year puts him into some dreadful stock that drops right through the floor. The fifth year, the customer calls the broker and says, "Look: I don't know about all these stocks we've been buying—I think maybe I'd be better off in bonds."

"Yeah, sure," says the broker, "but what do I know about bonds?"

—Old joke

I went to the track for the first time in my life last summer; to Belmont Park. I went with a fellow a few years my senior who's been going to the track twice a week for 20 years. This is a man who knows horses. I know absolutely nothing about horses, but I brought $100 and figured I'd learn. About the only part I really understood were the hot dogs and beer, but the hot dogs weren't running and my midweek afternoon limit is three beers, so by the sixth race I was getting kind of bored and decided it was high time to place a bet.

My friend showed me the lineup for the race, explained why Such and Such would almost surely win, and reacted with ill-disguised derision when I said, no, I wasn't going to put my money on Such and Such, I was going to put my money on Willow. Willow? Willow, he chided, had never even raced before and had absolutely nothing going for her. (Or him. I never did get that straight.) She was the kind of horse they put in the race so none of the other horses would have to finish last. "You're missing the point," I explained. "Willow is going off at 25 to 1."

My friend tried to tell me about sucker bets and all that

(the odds at the track are always against you, but they're against you worst on the long shots), but I went and placed my bet and came back to our box and began trying to figure out where the race was going to start from. All the races had been starting from different points on the track, which was calibrated in furlongs, and I had been having some difficulty training my rented binoculars on the proper stretch of grass.

"And they're off!" announced the stationmaster (I recognized his voice from the Penn Station P.A. system), and I am asking—"Where?"

Even after I found them I couldn't really tell the horses apart, but according to the stationmaster *Willow was in the lead*. I looked over at my friend, who had a knowing and slightly bored pucker to his face, and then back to try to find the horses. And Willow, according to the voice, *was still in the lead*.

I am ordinarily rather quiet among 15,000 strangers, but I had, after all, put my money on this horse, and I had, after all, consumed three fairly large beers. I began to shout, "Come onnnn, WILLow!" And Willow, at the half (or whatever they call it), was *still* in the lead.

Now, you think I am going to tell you that, with just a few yards to go, or something, Willow stumbled, or Willow punked out, or Willow got kicked by one of the other horses. But no—Willow won!

At 25 to 1, Willow won!

Unfortunately, I had bet only $3 of my $100 on Willow.

The point of all this—and I think you know it instinctively, but I'll spell it out anyway—is that if I had bet the full $100 on Willow, Willow would surely have lost. There is no way in the world she would have won.

Is there anyone who doubts this? Think about it.

People say: "One great speculation is worth a lifetime of prudent investing"—a terrific line, and true. The problem comes in finding the great speculation. Few people ever do, particularly if they are amateurs.

The line I prefer: "In the financial marketplace, you get

what you pay for, if you're careful. If you try to get more, you get burned.''

Savings accounts and government bonds and money-market funds are for the chicken-hearted. But I respect the right to be chicken-hearted. As you can perhaps tell from my Belmont stakes, I am rather chicken-hearted myself.

When prices are rising like yeast, it is tempting to abandon one's conservative ways and look for an investment vehicle that will rise in value at least as fast. But the chicken-hearted way to beat inflation is to *eat* at McDonald's, not invest in it.

Really, the challenge of chicken-hearted investing isn't deciding where to put your money, but resisting the temptation to put it elsewhere. *Face it: sure things are boring.* Treasury bills have terribly predictable plots that make lousy cocktail party conversation (even if they do have some redeeming snob appeal), and they won't make you rich. If the United States Treasurer really wanted to sell those bills, she would issue them at slightly lower interest rates—and put the difference into a kitty for which there would be a daily drawing. The United States Lottery. That would give Treasury bill buyers something to check in the paper every day and a chance—however thin—to strike it rich.

Once in a long while you do find a sure thing with an outsized payoff, but it is very rare. The only time I was ever so fortunate was years ago, with a stock called Nation-Wide Nursing Centers. Of course, under normal circumstances nursing home stocks are not fare for the chicken-hearted. But this was one of those rare sure things. Through some remarkable good luck, on a day when this stock was selling for $22 a share over-the-counter—that was the price you would have paid—*I* was able to snag 500 shares at just $8 each, "under-the-counter." The only hitch was that the shares were unregistered, which meant I couldn't sell them for a while. It was a virtual gift of $7,000, which was hard enough to believe, let alone turn down.

Ordinarily, however, there is no such thing as a financial bargain. The financial markets are too large and efficient for that. By and large, as I've said, if you're careful, you get what you pay for. Try to get more and you generally get what's coming to you. I was told I would have to hold my nursing home stock for three months, when it would almost surely be bought out by a merger-mad steel company at $40 a share. The head of research for one of Wall Street's most prestigious firms was in the deal for 4,000 shares, so I knew this was on the up and up.

The stock is now zero, and I am still expecting to hear from that steel company any day.

There are two kinds of money in the world, debt and equity. Debt is an IOU; equity is a piece of the action. Debt is bonds or bills or notes or savings accounts—anything where you *lend* your money, whether to the U.S. government, a local government, a savings bank, a corporation—whomever. (Yes, when you deposit money in a savings bank, you are actually lending the bank money. The bank is in your debt and must pay you interest. You have taken their IOU in exchange for your cash.) Equity is where you *invest* your money, with no promise that your investment will be recouped, but with the idea that as the company prospereth or falleth into decline, so shall you prosper or fall. (Actually, it's not that simple. The company may prosper while its stock falls and falls and falls. But we'll get to that.)

Until you have $5,000 or $10,000 someplace safe and liquid, like a savings account, unless you are so wealthy you don't have to worry about the contingencies of everyday living, like losing your job, you are crazy even to consider making riskier investments. Or more sophisticated ones. Relax: You are doing just the right thing. You are missing no great opportunities. You are *not* a sap. There is a time and a place for everything, and when cocktail party conversation turns to "investments," or "the market," I suggest the time has come for you to be smug. Let the others do what they do, say what they say—you are above it. They may gamble, they may speculate, they may talk of doubling their money (and not mention halving it); you are smug. (See pages 170–71 for a set of smug rejoinders and harmless financial one-liners to keep up your end of the conversation.)

The television campaign the savings bank people used to run about commercial banks being for businesses, while savings banks are for people—"and I'm a people"—is so silly as not to bear discussion. But the other one you may have seen, which shows a man recounting his sad history of investment failures, and then has him brightening to say that now his money is in a savings account—he's "found a better way"—that one may be equally simpleminded, but it's really not such bad advice. The first several thousand dollars of anybody's money (aside from equity in a home) should be in a checking or savings account (or a money-market mutual fund, which is essentially the same thing). And for many people, that's *all* their money.

In choosing among savings accounts that provide checks and checking accounts that pay interest and money-market funds that do both but are not federally insured—and whatever else of this sort the financial community may devise—the important thing to remember is: It doesn't make much difference.

By and large, the going rate for safe, liquid funds will be about the same everywhere. One bank may offer a bit more than another for a while; money market funds may offer more—because this is the principal basis on which they can compete—but be a little less convenient (and downright uncomprehending if you ever go to them asking for a home improvement loan); credit unions may offer a slightly better deal because they are nonprofit.

You want your account, or accounts, someplace convenient that provides good service. (There's something

to be said for doing much or all of your banking business
with one institution in order to build a good relationship.)

The danger is that you will spend so much time trying to
figure out whether the 9% checking account with the $4
monthly fee but no charge for checks is a better deal than
the 8¾% savings account with no fee but a 20 cent charge
for each check or deposit (answer: choose the one with the
closest cash machine) that you will lose sight of the larger
issues. For the real question is not how to wring an extra
1% out of the $5,000 or $10,000 you keep completely safe
and liquid. An extra 1% on $5,000 or $10,000 comes to
$50 or $100 a year—after taxes, perhaps just $25 or $50.
You are too busy to spend much time worrying about $50.
The real question is that of overall strategy: What proportion of your assets do you want to keep completely safe
and liquid? What proportion might you prudently tie up for
a while to get a higher return? Two years? Ten years?
Thirty years? What proportion should you risk in the stock
market to get a higher return still? What proportion should
be in tax-free securities? Or in real estate? How well are
you diversified?

The books that really used to get me, back in the days
when all any small saver could earn was 5½%, no matter
what, and no saver of any size had even dreamed of
double-digit rates, were the ones they advertised that prom-
ised to tell you "HOW TO MAKE UP TO 13½% OR MORE
ON YOUR SAVINGS—ALL FULLY INSURED!" The ads ran
on to say how upset the savings banks were about this
book, but there was nothing they could do, and the interest
you earned could be even more than 13½%, etc., etc. And
when you sent for the book—could you really have expected differently?—you found that to earn these astounding
rates of interest you had to spend most of your waking life
transferring money with split-second precision from one
bank on a Friday afternoon to another that handled its
accounting a different way, and back and forth and around—
*and even then you were only earning this rate a few days
out of the year*. You did *not* earn 13% annually. Most of

the time you earned just 5½%, or whatever was the going rate; *sometimes* you could jigger it to earn at a 13% annual rate over a long weekend. That sort of thing. (In the meantime, you could have been earning 8% or so continuously, in a long-term savings account.) And for those extra dimes and nickels over the weekend—*who cares?*

One such book was advertised several years ago—full-page ads in reputable magazines, for months—as being available only by mail, at $8.98. In fact, a 95-cent paperback edition was available in stores while the ad was running. The author told me: "After reading the huckster's copy on my book, you wonder whether they're the same books! The way they're advertised—I know if I bought one, I'd be steaming mad." Nonetheless, he wrote at least one more such book for the same publisher.

If, then, you have $10,000 or less, you know what to do with it. You've probably already done it: It's earning interest someplace safe. If this book hasn't made a dime for you, at least it's confirmed your good sense. And you can always start reading again when your fortunes swell. (Well, do read the next chapter, because you may be able to salt away and compound your savings tax-free.)

For those who have got enough money to make an extra point or two of interest worth worrying over, there are three things that will determine what you can get for it, three things the financial markets reward: volume, patience, and risk. To each of the three, the same refrain dolefully applies: the rich get richer.

Volume. As with any product, financial or otherwise, if you buy in quantity, you get discount prices. To buy and sell 20 shares of AT&T costs the little guy roughly 6% in commissions. To buy and sell 2,000 shares costs Big Money half a percent. Similarly, the modest $25 service charge Merrill Lynch levies on a purchase of $10,000 90-day Treasury bills cuts the effective annual interest rate by a full 1%. There is no service charge at Merrill Lynch on T-bill transactions of $50,000 or more.

It is well known that the odds are worst for the little guy—whether it be the dreadful odds of the state lotteries or the only slightly less dreadful odds of the nickel slot machines. The smaller the stakes, the larger the cut the house demands.

Patience. The longer you are willing to tie up your money, the higher the interest rate you will ordinarily be paid for it. (During occasional "credit crunches," short-term rates may temporarily exceed long-term rates.) One reason for this is that the future is unpredictable, so the further into it you tie up your money, the more you are being exposed to the third variable:

Risk. The more risk you take, the greater your potential reward (and the greater your chance of loss—see the graph). But how much risk—even if it is, in your opinion, a "good" risk—can you afford to take?

The Only Graph in This Book

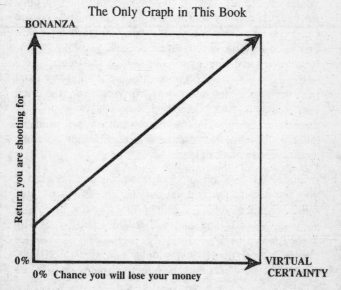

If I offered you 2-to-1 odds on the flip of an honest coin—heads you win $20, tails you lose $10—wouldn't you take the bet? But what if the odds were the same, only you stood to lose $1,000? Or $50,000? Wherever you draw the line is one measure of your chicken-heartedness—which is doubtless justified. There are a lot of excellent risks around that people of limited means just cannot prudently accept.

One of them may be the stock market, but that's another chapter. For now, what are the alternatives for the investor who wants to take only minimal risk?

Broadly speaking, these financial "instruments," also called "debt instruments," can be divided into short- and long-term—just as your own credit card borrowings are short-term, while your mortgage seems to stretch on into eternity.

Short-term Instruments

For short-term investment with maximum safety, the most practical, convenient alternative is your local bank, credit union, or one of the money-market mutual funds.

Money-market funds merge your initial deposit (minimum $1,000 to $5,000, depending on the fund) with hundreds of millions of dollars more and then invest it in blue-chip short-term government and corporate obligations such as U.S. Treasury bills (denominated in $10,000s and issued with 3-, 6-, 9-, and 12-month maturities); commercial paper (denominated in $100,000s or more and issued like IOUs for short periods by major corporations); "c.d.'s" (certificates of deposit issued by banks, denominated in $100,000s or more); and soon-to-mature government agency bonds, World Bank bonds, and Treasury notes or Treasury bonds.* You are credited with your share of the interest daily and can withdraw any amount at any time (or, in some cases, after 15 days). You can write

---

*The difference between Treasury bills, bonds, and notes is the length of time for which they are issued. Treasury bills have maturities up to 1 year; Treasury notes have maturities from 1 year to 10; Treasury bonds are issued with maturities of more than 10 years.

checks on your account, subject to certain minimums, usually at no charge—and your money will continue earning interest in the fund until the check actually clears. Unlike bank accounts, the funds aren't federally insured, but the securities they buy entail very little risk.

You can read a whole book about money-market funds (William Donoghue's *Complete Guide to Money-Market Funds*, $13.95), but you really have just three choices: most of the funds, which are all about the same; some of the funds, which pay a shade less interest because they invest only in completely safe government bonds; and a few of the funds, which specialize in tax-free bonds and so offer a lower yield that is exempt from federal income tax. *Money* runs a listing of the major funds and what they yield each month; *Barron's* and the *Wall Street Journal* are filled with ads for them; or call the mutual fund "families" whose toll-free numbers are listed on pages 175–76.

The most convenient money-market funds for substantial investors are the cash management accounts—CMA's—pioneered by Merrill Lynch and now offered by a great many brokers. Here your cash balances are automatically swept into a money-market checking account that also allows you to trigger automatic margin loans against the value of the securities in your account. What's more, some CMA's allow you to code your checks by category. At year's end, you get an organized printout and tally of all your tax-deductible expenditures.

Most substantial investors in the future are likely to have at least one such account along with a money-market checking account at their bank.

Long-term Instruments—Background

When you buy a bond you are lending money, whether to Uncle Sam, General Motors, or the City of Houston. There are three risks involved in buying a bond. The first is that you won't get paid back. The second is that you will get paid back early. The third is that, should you want to sell the bond some time before maturity (the payback date), you won't be able to get as much for it as you paid.

The first risk is a function of the creditworthiness of the borrower. If you're lending your money to the federal government, or even to most local governments and major corporations, you have little to worry about. If you're lending to an entity that is a bit touch-and-go—New York City, Chrysler, most airlines—you do have something to worry about, but you will be paid to worry.

Happily, you need not spend more than a few minutes investigating the creditworthiness of the entities whose bonds you are considering. This is done *for* you in two ways. First, every major bond is rated by two rating services, Standard & Poor's and Moody's. *Their* men in green eyeshades pore over balance sheets and tax bases and quick ratios and coverage ratios—and reduce it all for you to schoolgrades. Triple-A (AAA) is the best. Anything with a *B* in it (Baa, for example) means "Beware"; it is *probably* OK, except this is the chapter about taking minimal risk and sleeping soundly at night, so stick to A-rated, or even double-A-rated, bonds, even though they pay a little less. (C-rated bonds are pure speculations.)

The folks at the rating services are not infallible, but their analyses are likely to be as astute as yours or mine, so why waste time duplicating their effort?

Even without checking the ratings, you can tell a lot about the quality of a bond just by looking at how its yield compares with the yields of other bonds. These are reasonably "efficient" markets, and you just are not going to find one Telephone bond that is way out of line with the rest, nor a General Motors bond that pays as well as an American Motors bond. If anything, you should shy away from bonds that pay exceptional interest: there is a reason why they pay so well.

(Really, you can get just about any interest rate you want. You want 10%? Here's a General Motors bond. You want 12%? Have some Commonwealth Edison. Fourteen percent? How about Rapid American? Sixteen percent? How about Eastern Airlines?)

If you are looking at corporate bonds, first check to see what IBM and GMAC and Exxon and the phone companies are yielding on bonds of similar maturity. You can probably afford to take a little more risk than this, and get a little higher return; but don't reach too far.

Also, because the world is highly uncertain, even for monoliths like the phone company, it is only prudent to diversify. Don't lend *all* your money to Pacific Telephone—the earthquake, or a breakthrough in mental telepathy, could ruin you.

Yet it doesn't pay to spread your money over *too* many different bonds, because the flip side of diversification is volume. Bonds are denominated in $1,000s,* but any order for fewer than ten or twenty at a time, while you can probably get it executed, is likely to cost an extra 1 or 2% or more in the spreads that bond dealers take for their trouble.

The second thing to watch out for in buying a bond is its "callability." Many bonds are issued with provisions that allow the issuer to call them in before maturity. When this happens, you get the full $1,000 face value of the bond—often with a small premium—but you then have to go out looking for a new place to lend your money. And since borrowers have a tendency to call their bonds when interest rates have fallen, you may be sorry you didn't buy a noncallable bond.

One way around this problem is to buy bonds that, although callable, were issued when interest rates were low, and so sell in the open market at a big discount from par. (The higher the general level of interest rates when you read this, the more deep discount bonds there will be.) If you buy a bond for $500 and it *is* called away from you

---

*Don't be confused by the way they are quoted—as a percentage of par ($1,000). A bond selling at 88¼—88¼% of par—costs $882.50; at 94½, $945.00; at 106⅜, $1,063.75.

ten years early at $1,000—well, I can think of worse things, can't you?

The third risk in buying bonds is that you may not be able to get back what you paid when you go to sell them—even though if you held on to maturity you would get the full $1,000 face value of each bond.

This third risk, the interest rate risk, is a function of the money market.

There is a market for money just as there is a market for everything else—coffee, plywood, lemons—and when lots of people are trying to borrow but few are willing to lend, the price—namely, interest rates—goes up. When few are trying to borrow and many are eager to lend, the price— interest rates—goes down. Simple supply and demand, plus a good dose of government intervention. (The government controls the overall supply of money—which unlike coffee, plywood, or lemons does not grow on trees.)

The key to everything financial, and to nearly every- thing economic, is interest rates. When the going rate for money rises, bond prices automatically (and stock prices almost as automatically) fall. When the going rate for money falls, bonds (and stocks) rise. There is nothing mysterious about this; it is simple arithmetic. If you paid $1,000 ("par") for a bond that paid $50 a year interest, and then interest rates went up such that newly issued bonds were paying $70 interest, who in his right mind would buy yours for $1,000? Why would anyone take 5% interest when the going rate has risen to 7%? If, however, you offered the bond at, say, $850, you might be able to sell it (depending on how long it had to run to maturity), because the buyer would be getting $50 interest on $850— 5.88%—*plus* the prospect of a $150 profit when the bond matured.

(On stock prices, interest rates have a triple-barreled effect. For one thing, the higher interest rates go, the less attractive stock dividends look by comparison . . . so people sell stocks to buy bonds, and stock prices fall until dividends *do* look attractive. Second, high interest rates discourage people from borrowing to buy stocks on margin. Third, high interest rates mean high costs to business and less incentive to invest, expand, employ—all the things that make the economy boom, profits flow, and stock prices climb.)

There are different interest rates for different kinds of borrowers and different kinds of loans, but they all move in rough tandem. If the rate banks charge their prime customers goes up, you can be sure the rates they charge their lesser customers will go up as well. If corporations have to pay more interest to float a bond issue, you can be sure municipalities do, too.

Interest rates, furthermore, sit on top of inflation. If inflation is generally expected to run at 6% a year, lenders are going to feel awfully foolish lending their money at 5%—so they don't. As a general rule of thumb, long-term interest rates on high-quality bonds run around 3% above lenders' expectations of long-term inflation rates.

For a bit of perspective, let alone nostalgia, see on the next page how interest rates have fluctuated since 1920. Up, mostly.

You will notice that someone who bought a 20-year 3% bond at face value ($1,000) when it was issued in 1955, entitling him to $30-a-year interest until 1975, probably began to feel regretful around the year 1957, when similar bonds were being issued at nearly 4%—$40-a-year interest. It is the same feeling one would have buying a TV set shortly before a greatly improved model was released.

Had one, on the other hand, bought 6% General Motors Acceptance Corp. bonds at $430 each in July 1982—bonds that promised to pay $60 a year until 2011—one could have turned around and sold them in January 1983 (having collected $30 in interest on each in the meantime) for $560 apiece. A 30% gain in six months.

Clearly, if you knew which way interest rates were going, you could profit many ways. Many people therefore try to guess, and some, in any given year, guess right. Few, however, can guess right consistently, least of all

A Table That Looks Boring
But Is Actually Most Revealing

Year	Prime Rate	Triple-A Bonds	Municipal Bonds	Savings Accounts	Home Mortgages	Inflation
1920	6.58%	6.12%	4.98%	4 %	5.75%	2.3%
1925	4.98	4.88	4.09	4	5.90	3.8
1929	6.02	4.73	4.27	4½	5.92	0
1930	3.50	4.55	4.07	4½	5.95	−6.0
1935	1.50	3.60	2.40	2½	5.26	3
1940	1.50	2.84	2.50	2	5.40	.1
1945	1.50	2.62	1.67	1½	4.70	2.3
1946	1.50	2.53	1.64	1½	4.74	18.2
1947	1.52	2.61	2.01	1½	4.80	9.0
1948	1.85	2.82	2.40	1½	4.91	2.7
1949	2.00	2.66	2.21	1½	4.93	1.8
1950	2.07	2.62	1.98	2	4.95	5.8
1951	2.56	2.86	2.00	2	4.93	5.9
1952	3.00	2.96	2.19	2½	5.03	.9
1953	3.17	3.02	2.72	2½	5.09	.6
1954	3.05	2.90	2.37	2½	5.15	− .5
1955	3.16	3.06	2.53	2¾	5.18	4
1956	3.77	3.36	2.93	2¾	5.19	2.9
1957	4.20	3.89	3.60	3	5.42	3.0
1958	3.83	3.79	3.56	3¼	5.58	1.8
1959	4.48	4.38	3.95	3¼	5.71	1.5
1960	4.82	4.41	3.73	3½	5.85	1.5
1961	4.50	4.35	3.46	3½	5.87	.7
1962	4.50	4.33	3.18	4	5.90	1.2
1963	4.50	4.26	3.23	4	5.84	1.6
1964	4.50	4.40	3.22	4	5.78	1.2
1965	4.54	4.49	3.27	4	5.74	1.9
1966	5.62	5.13	3.82	4	6.14	3.4
1967	5.63	5.51	3.98	4	6.33	3.0
1968	6.28	6.18	4.51	4	6.83	4.7
1969	7.95	7.03	5.81	4	7.66	6.1
1970	7.91	8.04	6.50	4¼	8.27	5.5
1971	5.70	7.39	5.70	4¼	7.59	3.4
1972	5.25	7.21	5.27	4¼	7.45	3.4
1973	8.02	7.44	5.18	5	7.95	8.8
1974	10.80	8.57	6.09	5¼	8.92	12.2
1975	7.86	8.83	6.89	5¼	8.75	7.0
1976	6.83	8.44	6.64	5¼	8.90	4.8
1977	6.82	8.20	5.68	5¼	8.68	6.5
1978	9.06	8.99	6.03	5¼	9.72	9.3
1979	12.67	10.05	6.52	5½	10.94	13.0
1980	15.27	12.77	8.60	5½	13.50	11.9
1981	18.87	15.48	11.33	5½	16.31	8.6
2/83	11.00	12.0	10.00	5½	13.25	3.9

you or I or the man on all-news radio. Experts disagree; and the majority view at any given time is about as likely to be wrong as the minority view. The one thing on which there is nearly unanimous agreement is the difficulty of predicting interest rates.

That notwithstanding, I pay particular attention to the opinions of Citibank, to which most of the world is in hock anyway, so they should know; and of *The Bank Credit Analyst,* which, at $425 a year, ought to have an idea, too.

Then I flip a coin.

Certainly rates in the fifties seemed very high by comparison to the forties—yet in the sixties rates climbed still higher. Almost no one in the world would have believed, in 1965, that a mere 15 years later interest rates would top 20% in the United States of America—which is why they were willing to buy long-term bonds that yielded less than 5%. I like to think we may not see such lofty rates again in our lifetimes. But by the time you read this—or by the next time you do—rates could be even higher. Or spiraling inflation could shatter the value of the currency altogether, as it did in Germany post–World War I, in which case *any* long-term fixed-income security becomes worthless. On the other hand, imagine having 14% Treasury bonds five years from now if inflation and interest rates fall back to the level of the fifties.

It becomes a question not so much of which high-quality borrower you want to lend your money to—that's easy, it doesn't matter—but of how long you are willing to get tied in to a particular rate.

The first answer, as with any other financial question, is to diversify. It makes little sense to put all your money into bonds of one maturity—say, 20-year bonds—any more than it makes sense to put all your money into one bond.

The second answer is that you are not an insurance company—founded in 1734 and not likely to founder much before 2234 (merge, maybe; founder, no)—and so, not having that kind of endless inflow of big dollars, nor institutional immortality, you should probably not tie up *too* much of your money in 30-year bonds. (You can always sell the bonds, of course, but if interest rates rise, you will sell at a loss.)

On the other hand, equity investments over the last 50 years haven't averaged out to return much more than 9% (dividends plus appreciation), so if the opportunity again arises to lock in a sure 14 or 15% for twenty or thirty years, with none of the bother or risk of choosing stocks—it will be tempting to do so.

We have become increasingly aware in this country that inflation of much more than 2% or 3%—or certainly 5%—is murderous. It drives up interest rates, eats away at profits, lowers living standards, stifles the incentive to invest, worsens unemployment. Runaway "double-digit" inflation is the economic equivalent of nuclear disaster, a thing that must be avoided at all costs—or so most economists and politicians believe—if the economic order is to survive. As a result, one expects a great deal of effort and energy to be applied at the highest levels to keep interest rates from reaching new peaks.

This was not nearly so much the case in the fifties and early sixties, when the rise in inflation and interest rates, while unwelcome, was not widely perceived to threaten the foundations of society. It was thought, in fact, that a little bit of inflation was a good thing. It made everyone feel prosperous—wages and profits and real estate values kept edging up—and the confidence that inspired helped to keep the economy bubbling along. But if inflation of 2% and long-term interest rates of 5% are well within the system's tolerance, double-digit inflation is something else again entirely. The difference can be sensed from the compound-interest tables (see pages 177–79), which grow fairly leisurely at 2 or 4%, but alarmingly at 8%, explosively at 12%, and beyond all imagining at 20%. In 30 years, $1 grows to $3.24 at 4% interest—and shrinks in buying power to 54 cents at 2% inflation, which may be more to the point. But at 12%, the dollar grows not three times as fast, but nine times as fast—to $29.96 in 30 years. And at 12% inflation it shrinks not to 54 cents but to 2 cents.

The prospect of $1 shrinking in value to 2 cents in 30 years is not one that encourages people or companies to invest their money in long-term projects. And without such investments, the productive machine eventually grinds to a halt. Capitalism fails.

Knowing this, union leaders, businessmen, bankers, and politicians alike are anxious to keep inflation and interest rates low enough, at least, to allow the system to survive. Hence, long-term interest rates are not likely to keep climbing in the eighties and nineties as they have, fairly steadily, since the thirties. It's hard to see how they could without the system's collapsing altogether. That is, of course, a much publicized possibility, but in that case not many other investments would fare much better than high-quality long-term bonds, anyway.

So much for background.

Long-term Instruments—Specifics

U.S. savings bonds are a better deal than they once were, now that rates on the new EE bonds are tied to 85% of Treasury note yields, with a 7.5% minimum and no maximum. But you won't get the full rate of interest if you fail to hold these ten-year bonds at least five years. Cash them in early and your interest will be calculated at rates ranging from 4% (if held six months) to 7¼% (if held four and a half years).

The bonds do offer tax advantages—interest is exempt from state and local taxes, and federal tax may be postponed until you cash them in—but if you need tax advantages, you should probably be in municipal bonds instead.

Municipal bonds. There are two kinds of bonds: most of them, which are taxable; and municipals, which are not. The interest on bonds issued by state and local governments, county sewage authorities and the like is federal income tax–free. You don't even have to report it. In most cases, it is also exempt from local taxes of the same region. New York City bonds, for example, are exempt from New York State and New York City income tax (but not from California income tax—California's bonds are). The table on page 50 compares the value of tax-free interest with taxable interest. The higher your marginal tax bracket, the more sense it makes for you to look for tax-free bonds.

(In addition to its "current yield," a bond selling for less than its $1,000 "face value" will, at maturity, provide you with an additional profit. That profit, if you've held the bond for a year or more, *is* taxed, but as a long-term capital gain.*)

If you are in the 35% tax bracket (and expect to remain there a while), and if you have taxable bonds in your closet, it's very hard to see why you shouldn't sell them and buy municipals instead. If you have to sell at a loss to do this all the better. The loss will lower your taxes.

It is possible that some day the tax-free status of municipals will be revoked—although I doubt it. That would just force local governments to pay higher rates for the money they borrow, which in turn would mean raising local taxes (or else seeking a federal subsidy, as has been proposed). But even if municipals did lose their tax exemption, it is almost inconceivable that the law would affect those bonds that had already been issued. More likely, the new law would affect only bonds issued thereafter. In which case, if anything, old municipals would likely *rise* in value, because there would be a limited and gradually shrinking pool of such bonds.

Caution: I know what you are thinking. Why not borrow money at 12%, which in the 50% tax bracket comes to only 6% after taxes, and use it to buy municipals that yield 10% tax-free? Make a profit without putting up a dime!

---

*A capital gain results when you sell something—be it a stock, a bond, or a horse—at a profit. If you have owned it a year or less, the profit is called a short-term capital gain, and is taxed just as if it were regular income. If you have owned it more than a year, it is a long-term capital gain and, under current law, only 40% of it is taxed.

It's a great idea, only Uncle Sam has thought of it, too. The IRS will disallow interest deductions if in its view the interest was incurred to obtain funds to buy tax-free bonds.

	A tax-free bond that yields . . .				
	4.0%	6.0%	8.0%	10.0%	12.0%
If your marginal tax bracket* is:	. . . is as good, after-tax, as a taxable investment that yields:				
0%	4.0%	6.0%	8.0%	10.0%	12.0%
10	4.4	6.7	8.9	11.1	13.3
20	5.0	7.5	10.0	12.5	15.0
25	5.3	8.0	10.6	13.3	16.0
30	5.7	8.6	11.4	14.3	17.1
35	6.2	9.2	12.3	15.4	18.5
40	6.7	10.0	13.3	16.7	20.0
45	7.3	10.9	14.5	18.2	21.8
50	8.0	12.0	16.0	20.0	24.0
55	8.9	13.3	17.8	22.2	26.7

*See chapter 2. If the bond you are considering is not exempt from your local income tax, then it is only your marginal federal income tax bracket that is relevant here.

Government bonds, issued by the U.S. government and its agencies, are both liquid and safe, except that if you want to sell them before they mature, and if interest rates have risen in the meantime, you will suffer a loss. For a listing of government bonds, when they mature, and what they are yielding, look in the back pages of the *Wall Street Journal*. At first the numbers and abbreviations may put you off, but the fog will clear. For each category of government or government agency bonds there will be listed a range of maturities, from bonds that mature this year to some that don't mature until the next century. You will notice that in each case—except during a credit crunch —the "yield" rises gradually with the maturity. Patience is rewarded.

Government bonds, unlike municipals, are fully taxed by the federal government but *not* subject to state or city taxes. They may be purchased through your commercial banker or your broker, although neither will be thrilled with the business: the commissions they charge on this kind of transaction are very low.

The real problem with government bonds is that the federal government is considered such a good risk—the bonds are *so* safe—they don't pay very good interest.

Take a chance. Lend at least some of your money to General Motors or AT&T and earn higher interest. (Unless you are in a high tax bracket, in which case it would make better sense to lend to a high-rated municipality.)

Although stockbrokers don't get rich from corporate or municipal bond commissions, either*—and will doubtless try to turn the conversation to stocks when you call, so beware—you should be able to get some advice from your local account representative concerning which bonds to buy. He can, for example, check out the call provisions of different bonds.

Mainly, however, you have to decide for yourself how much risk to take; over how many different bonds to spread that risk; and how long you are willing to wait to redeem the bonds at par value.

There are bond mutual funds—both **corporate bond funds** and tax-free **municipal bond funds**—that do the choosing for you and provide much greater diversification than you ever could. However, some charge sales commissions or redemption fees, and all charge management fees. Unless that management fee is awfully low (½% or less), as a few are, it's hard to justify paying it.

It's one thing to pay a management fee to one of the short-term money-market funds described earlier: for that fee you get a fair amount of service as you move your

---

*Brokers typically charge around $5 to buy or sell a bond. Brokerage commissions for buying or selling an equivalent amount of stock can be four or five times as much.

money in and out, and you get an opportunity to participate in instruments denominated in enormous amounts you could never afford yourself. But with corporate or municipal bonds you plan to buy once and hold a long time, the management fees are harder to justify. It's just as easy to call a broker and buy ten bonds each in five different issues—$50,000 worth in all, on which the total commission should be about $250—as it is to purchase shares in a bond fund and then pay as much as 1%—$500—*year after year* as a management fee. As for expertise in choosing the bonds, you may be able to tell the difference between AAA and Baa almost as well as an expert.

Dreyfus had a tax-exempt bond fund that charged up to 0.95% in annual management fees in the years when high-quality municipals yielded as little as 5%. Taking nearly 1% off the top meant skimming off nearly a fifth of the tax-free income you would have gotten if you had bypassed the fund and bought bonds directly through a broker. (Your broker's firm should have a municipal bond expert on staff, too, if it makes you feel any better.)

Unit trusts are bond mutual funds that are *not* managed. Whatever corporate or municipal bonds the trust starts out with are the bonds which, barring any defaults, are eventually redeemed at the other end. As a result, there is no management fee to speak of. There is generally a sales commission, however, of from 2.5 to 4.5%.

Unit trusts are put together with different maturities. They can be found advertised in such papers as *Barron's* and the *Wall Street Journal*. They do provide diversification. However, some of the trusts will accept risks, such as hospital bonds backed solely by the revenue of the hospital (and not by the taxing power of the city or county it is located in), that you yourself might not. The man who assembles the package of bonds is more concerned that the yield look attractive, so it sells, than that 12 years from now, when he is long gone, the bonds remain safe.

Once sold to the public, unit trusts are not traded.

Investors may redeem their shares with the trustee at "net asset value"—at a loss if bond prices have fallen since the trust was issued, at a profit if they have have risen.

Convertible bonds pay a specified interest rate, but also give you the right to convert your bonds into a given number of shares of common stock. That's what's known as an "equity kicker." With a convertible bond, you have a chance to both sleep *and* eat well. In tough times, unless the company goes bankrupt altogether, you still get your interest; but should the company strike it rich, you could profit along with the common shareholders.

Preferred stocks are like bonds—they pay a fixed dividend— but they never "mature." They are like a permanent loan and not, as their name implies, a piece of the action. They are "preferred" only in that their dividend must be paid in full before any dividend on common stock may be paid; and if the company fails, preferred shareholders come ahead of common shareholders—but behind an awful lot of others, such as bondholders—if anything remains to be split up. What preferreds do not provide is an opportunity to participate in the company's good fortune, should it have any (unless it is a "convertible preferred"). The dividend never goes up.

A "cumulative preferred" is one that promises to pay its dividend no matter what, even if it can't be paid on time. The dividend may be omitted if necessary, but it is still owed to the preferred stockholders, and no common-stock dividends may be paid until all the preferred dividends are paid off. In the case of a company that flirted with bankruptcy for a few years, the arrearage could be substantial—and an investor who gambled on the preferred at giveaway prices could profit handsomely if the company ever righted itself. LTV Corp., the steel-meatpacking-aerospace conglomerate, which is still not the world's most financially sound, has a $5 cumulative convertible preferred which once sold for as much as $202 a share (1967), but which you could have bought a few years later

(1971) for $17. The dividends had stopped—but they were "cumulating," should the company ever recover. In 1975, $22.50 a share in back dividends was paid out to the then preferred shareholders, and the $5 dividend was resumed. Today it sells for $46.

Of course, this kind of speculation is hardly what you would call minimal risk.

By and large, preferred stocks are not good investments for individuals. One reason is that *corporate* investors bid them up in price. To corporations, but not individuals, preferreds provide an important tax advantage, and hence are worth a premium. Why should *you* pay a premium for a tax break that doesn't apply to you?

One reason to do so is that unlike a high-yielding bond, which may promise to pay its high interest for "only" ten years (after which it may be callable), with preferred stocks you can lock in a high yield *forever*. Presuming, that is, that (*a*) the preferred isn't callable (some are, so you've got to check), and (*b*) the issuer remains in business forever.

None of this would have much mattered until recently. With the benefit of hindsight, at least, who would have wanted to lock in 6 or 8% forever? But if the relentless long-term upward trend in interest rates has finally reversed, as it conceivably may have, then it's not such a bad thing to lock in current rates forever.

I don't pretend to know where long-term interest rates will be in five years, or 20, but on the chance they'll be appreciably lower, I bought some preferreds for my Keogh Plan last year that yield 14%.

I also bought some **zero-coupon bonds**. These are bonds that, curiously enough, pay no interest. Instead, they're sold cheap and rise gradually to $1,000 at maturity. The typical zero, maturing in twelve years at $1,000, might be sold for $250. To grow from $250 to $1,000 in twelve years is to grow at 12¼% a year.

The longer the maturity of the bonds, the lower their

price. I bought one that sold for $51.25. It promised a nearly twenty-fold appreciation of my principle in 30 years. What fun to see the $100,000 face value show up on my brokerage statement each month! Over the next thirty years, the market value of those bonds (I bought 100 of them) should rise from $5,125, which I paid, to $100,000, which I'm supposed to be paid back.

Purchasers of ordinary long-term bonds may lock in high interest—but what will they earn in interest *on that*? That's the beauty of a zero-coupon bond: assuming the issuer doesn't go broke, the compounded annual return is locked in from the start.

A broker can give you a list of zeroes to choose from, some of them traded on the New York Stock Exchange. The ones McDonalds issued are called Money-Multipliers. The ones Merrill Lynch issued, tied to Treasury securities, are called TIGERS. Salomon Brothers copied them with "CATS." GMAC and Allied Corp. and TransAmerica and Pepsico are among those that have issued zeroes.

The big disadvantage of zeroes is that they're taxed. Never mind that you're getting no interest; says the IRS: if the bond is geared to appreciate at 10½% a year, then, by damn, you're going to pay tax (ordinary income tax) as if you'd gotten 10½% in interest.

So zeroes—except *municipal* zeroes, of which there are a few, too—are a crummy investment for people who pay taxes. *But they're dandy for IRAs and Keogh Plans*, which are shielded from tax.

Let's say you buy for your IRA $2,000 of some stock or bond that throws off $108 in income every six months. What are you supposed to do with that $108? It's a nuisance, and much too small a chip to reinvest effectively.* With zeroes, there's no interest to worry about; they just keep compounding. What's more, $2,000 in cash can buy a respectable $10,000 or $20,000 or even $40,000 in bonds— money that will be waiting for you in 30 years.

---

* Unless you've bought shares in a mutual fund, in which case your income can be automatically reinvested.

Zeroes have another advantage. Most are "call protected." What sort of lunatic corporate treasurer, after all, would call in bonds at par ($1,000) that are selling at some tiny fraction thereof? *Some* zeroes, however, are callable according to special "accretion schedules" outlined in their prospectuses, so instead of seeing your money compound at 11% a year for 30 years, the music might stop after just five or ten. Ask your broker to check before you buy such a bond, or call the Treasurer's office of the corporation or municipality issuing it.

The final caution is that while some zeroes trade fairly actively and are listed in the paper every day, many do not. You'll always be able to sell, but you may not be offered the world's fairest price. And as with any long-term bond, when interest rates shoot up, bond prices fall.

Tax-deferred annuities are offered by insurance companies as a means of setting up retirement funds for people who can't set up the kinds of plans described in the next chapter.

Under such plans, you are paid a relatively high rate on your savings—*but the rate could fall once you've been hooked in the program*. It is often not guaranteed beyond the first year. In addition to their paying only a modest interest rate, the insurance companies charge either a sales fee at the outset or a redemption fee when you want out. Your money compounds without your having to pay tax on it until you withdraw it, presumably at retirement, when you will be in a lower tax bracket.

If you bought municipals instead, your money would not earn as high a rate (at least not initially), but neither would you *ever* have to pay taxes on it, nor any sales or redemption fee.

If you are in a high enough tax bracket, have your life insurance agent explain the additional features of the "single-premium deferred annuity contract," as it is called—but think twice before buying.

IMPORTANT NOTE:

Getting a high rate of interest doesn't help if you don't save money in the first place. Many people won't save unless "forced" to. For this reason, a payroll-savings plan or whole life insurance contract, or some other form of poor-return saving (for years savings bank Christmas Clubs paid no interest at all!) may be better than planning to buy bonds or stocks and never getting around to it.

What's more, not all payroll-savings plans are to be sniffed at. Sixty of the 100 largest industrial companies in the U.S. offer some form of payroll-savings plan, with the savings typically being invested either in savings bonds or the company's own stock. Not only do such plans enjoy tax advantages, *in more than half the cases the companies themselves kick in 50 cents or $1 for each $1 the employee contributes!* If your employer is so generous, by all means take full advantage of it. You can be sure no bank or broker is going to give you 50 cents outright for each dollar you save!

CHAPTER 4

The People's Loophole

If I had put just two million into that deal, I'd be a rich man today.

— A real estate man we know

If you have young children, here is one good way to have your savings compound tax-free:

Save money in *their* names, with their Social Security numbers on the savings or brokerage accounts, and let *them* pay taxes on the interest or dividends that accrue. As most six-year-olds are in the zero percent tax bracket, there will be no tax due on the first $1,000 or so of interest or dividends. Their savings for college will mount tax-free.*

Each parent can give each child up to $10,000 a year without having to pay gift tax. Of course, the money then belongs to the children, both interest and principal. But if you were going to spend it on them anyway, for law school, what difference does it make?

As custodian of a child's savings or brokerage account, you have the right to withdraw funds at any time to spend on the child's behalf (except that if you use the income from the account to support the child, the IRS may tax you as if you, not the child, had earned it). Or you can leave the money in savings certificates, stocks, or bonds to grow. The child may *not* touch the money—only the custodian may. You are not required to relinquish custodianship of the accounts until the child turns 18 or 21, depending on your state's age of maturity, but may do so sooner if you wish.

---

* You may obtain a Social Security number for your child from your local Social Security Administration office. All you need is the child's birth certificate. Filing a tax return for the child each year—which you must do—is also a very simple matter.

If you were in the 40% tax bracket and saved $1,000 a year for 18 years at 10% interest in your children's names, your $18,000 would have accumulated $27,599 in compounded after-tax interest—versus just $12,905 if you saved the money in your own name.

Either way, you set aside $1,000 a year; this way you come out $14,694 ahead. Just by doing your bookeeping a little differently.*

Or try this (at least in 1983 you could still try it; who knows when the IRS will crack down):

You want to take a short-term capital gain, but you're loathe to see it halved by taxes. So you sell the asset *at cost* to someone whose tax bracket is very low, like your daughter, and you let her (or her guardian) sell it on the open market. You've broken even on the sale; your daughter has realized a short-term capital gain. In her bracket, there's little or no tax due. Yes, there is a "gift" element in the bargain price at which you sold the stock; but no gift tax is due unless the gain that you're sheltering is in five figures, in which case you should check all this with your accountant anyway.

Or this: Make a non-interest-bearing loan to your child, repayable on demand. The interest you forgo is considered a gift to the child; the interest he or she earns is taxed at his or her low rate; you can demand repayment whenever you want. They're not bad loopholes, but this chapter is about an even better set, having to do with your retirement. *Even if you are still just a college student, earning several hundred dollars a year, I urge you to read this section.* If you wait until you're nearing retirement, it will be too late.

First the bad news:

As you doubtless know, all the money you've been paying in Social Security taxes, lo these many years, has not been set aside for your retirement. It has been paid out to people who are already in retirement. It's gone. The way the system works, when your golden years roll around,

---

* If you already have substantial assets, you might prefer to set up what is known as a Clifford Trust. The income from the trust goes to the child and is taxed at his rate, but the principal reverts back to you after ten years or more. Ask your accountant or attorney about this.

some other generation of workers will be paying taxes to support you. Which is fine except for two things. First, even at current levels Social Security benefits are more peanut butter than caviar. Second, by the time today's 30- and 40-year-olds are ready to retire, the population of this country will have shifted dramatically: Instead of having lots of workers working to support relatively few retirees—as things stand now—you are going to have relatively few under-65s working to support hordes of retirees. It's hard to see how even the current level of support will be maintained.

What this means is that if we want to live nicely, we will all have to provide, in large measure, for ourselves. The good news is that Congress has made it a lot easier for us to do so. Although ERISA, the pension reform act of 1974, is the most complicated law ever written—bureaucracy and the legal system run wild—it boils down to this: If you already have a pension plan where you work, you are less likely to get screwed out of your share of its benefits than you once were; and in any event you can now start a retirement plan of your own.

There are two kinds. If you earn any income, you may set up an Individual Retirement Account (IRA). If you have income from self-employment, you may set up a Keogh Plan, as well.

There are very few truly good things in the world, but if you qualify, these are two of them. In fact, anyone who qualifies to set up a Keogh Plan or IRA and doesn't is making a very big mistake.

With either plan, the income you contribute each year is exempted from taxes. So, too, the interest, dividends, and capital gains those contributions accrue. It is only when you begin withdrawing money from the plan, any time after you are 59½, that you pay taxes on what you take out. But by then, the assumption is, you are likely to be retired or semiretired and so in a relatively low tax bracket. Even if you're not, your savings will have been allowed to compound much faster than they otherwise could have.

Let's say you are 29½ and you contribute $1,000 to a

Keogh Plan or IRA next week. At 10% it would compound to $17,449 by the time you were 59½. Then, when you withdrew it—particularly if you had just retired and weren't earning much other taxable income—perhaps 30% of what you withdrew would go to taxes, leaving you with $12,214.

If you had *not* contributed that $1,000 to a Keogh Plan or IRA when you earned it, aged 29½, the first thing that would have happened is that it would have been taxed. If you were in the 40% bracket, $400 would immediately have gone to the government, leaving you $600. If you had then invested that $600 at the same 10% a year, it would have grown—after taxes—at just 6%. Thirty years later, aged 59½—assuming you had resisted the temptation to blow the money on a terrific Caribbean cruise or a bogus cosmetics franchise—it would have grown to $3,446.

The first way you are left with $12,214; the second way, a mere $3,446. The Keogh Plan or IRA leaves you with more than three times as much money after tax, even though it requires absolutely no more to start with, no more risk or effort, and, in fact, *less* self-discipline. (Because once it's locked up in the plan, you will not constantly be tempted to do something different with it.)

If you put that $1,000 into such a plan at age 25 instead of 29½, and waited to begin withdrawing it until you were 70½ instead of 59½, under the same assumptions the Keogh Plan or IRA would leave you with more than $49,691 after-tax, versus just $8,503.

And that's just $1,000, one year. If you contribute that much—or more—year after year, you are talking hundreds of thousands of dollars, as the table on the next page shows.

The prime thing to note from this table is the importance of starting early. Indeed, the contributions in your later years will add relatively little to the value of your fund. It is the early contributions which, compounded over time, grow enormously. You could, for example, contribute $1,000 a year from age 20 to 35 and then nothing. If you then withdrew the money between the ages of 65 and 80, your initial $15,000 would have grown (at 8% interest) to provide you well over $400,000!

If you assume your money will compound at *10%*, then that initial $15,000 will provide you with more than $1 million in your old age. At 12%? Nearly $3 million. The problem, of course, is that the higher the rate of return you assume, the higher the rate of inflation you should assume, too. So $3 million may not buy that much. Still, under just about any combination of assumptions, the double-barreled tax advantage of these plans—being able to deduct your contributions now and then to watch your money compound tax-free until it is withdrawn—is dramatic.

So why doesn't everyone who qualifies for such a plan set one up and contribute to it to the maximum extent allowed? The primary objection comes from people who don't want to tie up their money so long. You may not

If you contribute $1,000 a year* to a Keogh or IRA for the next . . .	. . . and if you can invest it at 8%, this is what you'll have, before taxes, when you begin withdrawing it:	Here's what the same savings would be worth, after taxes, without Keogh or IRA (assuming you are in the 40% bracket):
1 year	$ 1,080	$ 629
5	6,335	3,461
10	15,645	7,835
15	29,323	13,366
20	49,421	20,356
25	78,951	29,195
30	122,341	40,369
35	186,097	54,494
40	279,774	72,351
45	417,417	94,925

NOTE: A crucial assumption here is a steadily available 8% rate of interest. If interest rates average even higher, the payouts will be higher; if lower, lower. *But no matter what interest rates are, tax-free interest will grow much faster than taxed interest!*

*To figure what would happen if you contributed $2,000 a year, just double all the numbers; $3,000, triple—and so forth.

withdraw money from either the Keogh Plan or IRA until you turn 59½ without incurring a "stiff penalty." For most of us, who can't even plan our finances two months in advance, let alone two decades, this seems hopelessly far off in the future.

Yet there are two very strong arguments against that objection. In the first place, you *can* withdraw money from these plans. The penalty is 10% of what you withdraw, all of which is then taxed as income (the 10% excise tax is *not* deductible). And—in the case of the Keogh Plan—you are disqualified from making contributions to the plan for five years. But you would have had to pay taxes on that income, anyway, if you hadn't put it into the plan—so that part isn't so terrible. And 10%, while indeed a stiff penalty, may not be much to pay for having been allowed to compound your savings—as well as the portion the government would have taken—tax-deferred for several years.

Second and most important: Do you plan to have *any* money saved up by the time you are 59½? *Any* net worth? *Anything* to supplement your Social Security and the generosity of your children? If so—and for most people the answer is an emphatic yes—it may as well be in the form of a tax-free retirement fund. *What can you lose by not paying taxes?*

Unquestionably, a great deal we cannot anticipate will occur over the time spans we are speaking of here. Tax laws are bound to change; U.S. currency could become worthless through spiraling inflation à la Germany in the twenties; we could all be wiped out by epidemic or holocaust. However, none of that is particularly relevant to the question of whether to set up a Keogh Plan or IRA. It is virtually indisputable that whatever investment decisions you make, it's better to make them tax-free than taxable. Further, it is highly unlikely that Congress, no matter what it does with the tax laws, would retroactively penalize the millions of voters who, in good faith, set up tax-deferred retirement funds.

Now down to specifics:

Who qualifies for a Keogh Plan? Anyone with income from self-employment. Doctors, lawyers, dentists, writers, moonlighting policemen, accountants, store owners, barbers, gardeners, free-lancers, consultants, actors, real estate brokers, independent salesmen, decorators, tutors, tennis instructors, photographers: anyone who earns money for himself—not for a boss or employer—by selling a product or service, and whose business is not incorporated. *Even if you have a salaried job, income you earn on the side, on your own, qualifies for a Keogh Plan.*

Who qualifies for an Individual Retirement Account? Anyone who earns money—*including* money from self-employment.

What if you're already covered by a pension plan at work? You can still set up an IRA.

How much can you contribute each year?

IRA: Up to 100% of your earnings each year, but currently not more than $2,000 ($2,250 if married to a nonworking spouse, provided that it be split between two separate IRAs—one for each of you—with no more than $2,000 contributed each year to either one).

Keogh: Up to 15% of your earnings from self-employment, but not more than $15,000, in 1983; up to 20% of your earnings, but not more than $30,000, in 1984 and thereafter. Despite the 15% limitation, *the first $750 of earnings from self-employment is all eligible for the plan,* so long as gross adjusted income from all sources for the individual in question does not exceed $15,000.

Note, by the way, that in figuring your "earnings," investment income such as dividends and interest does not count. Also, if you are a dentist who grosses $50,000 a year but deducts $20,000 of expenses directly related to dentistry, your self-employment income is $30,000 for the purposes of figuring your maximum allowable contribution, not $50,000.

Must you contribute that much each year? No. As long as you do not exceed the maximums allowed, you can contribute as much or as little as you want each year.

What if you contribute more? You can be fined a penalty of 6% of the excess plus interest—and, of course, that portion of your tax deduction will be disallowed.

Can you contribute to both a Keogh Plan and an IRA in the same year? Yes.

What if you're married? All the better. Even though you may file your taxes jointly, there is no such thing as a joint IRA or Keogh Plan. He has his, she has hers. An otolaryngologist married to an anaesthesiologist could each deduct up to $2,000 a year for an IRA and up to $30,000 (after 1983) for a Keogh Plan to shelter a total of $64,000 a year.

Or take a more modest example. You are a salaried employee who puts $2,000 each year into an IRA. You'd like to put away more, and you can afford to (you make $52,000 a year), only you don't qualify for a Keogh Plan. But your spouse earns $2,400 a year as an occasional translator. (The federal government doles out documents to part-time translators all over the country.) So your spouse puts $2,000 of the $2,400 into an IRA, $400 into a Keogh Plan. Presto—your retirement contribution for the year (and your tax deduction) is more than twice as great: $4,400 instead of just $2,000. Repeated over 25 or 30 years, a difference of hundreds of thousands of dollars.

What if your spouse is unemployed? You can set up a "spousal IRA," to increase the limit on IRA contributions from $2,000 to $2,250. But let's say you are a plumber with your own IRA and Keogh Plan. Why not hire your spouse for $40 a week to handle your record keeping? Your joint income neither increases nor decreases, of course; but suddenly your spouse is eligible to sock away up to $2,000 a year into an IRA of her (or his) own.

When do you set up the plan? Today or tomorrow would be the best time, but with a Keogh Plan you have until the last day of the year. With an IRA, you have until April 15 of the *following* year.

When do you contribute to the plan? Once the paper work is done to set it up, you may contribute whenever you like during the year—in one lump sum or in many small payments—so long as you don't exceed the maximum allowable contribution. In fact, because it is hard to know just how much that will be until you've done your taxes, you actually have until you file your taxes the following year to make your contribution. However, the sooner you put money into the plan each year, the sooner it begins earning tax-free interest. Over the years this can mount up into a difference of tens or even hundreds of thousands of dollars. It is a good idea to contribute early—even January 2—as much as you feel confident of being allowed to, and then make a final contribution to bring you up to the limit when you know exactly how high that limit is.

How much should you contribute? The maximum allowable, if you can afford it. Not to do so is like throwing money away—unless you enjoy paying taxes. It may even be prudent, if your basic earning power is good, to *borrow* some of the cash you need to take full advantage of the Keogh or IRA deduction. The interest on your loan is tax-deductible (assuming you itemize your deductions) whereas the interest that that money will earn is tax-deferred. Don't borrow at usurious rates (as at a finance company); and in any case don't lock away savings you might need for emergencies or other essentials. But to pay interest for a few months, tax-deductibly, in order to take the fullest possible tax deduction for your retirement fund makes eminent good sense.

Is there any carryover provision? No. Even if you contribute less than you're entitled to one year, that does not entitle you to exceed the limit another year. It's now or never.

Must contributions be in cash? Yes. But that doesn't mean you can't sell your 50 shares of GM (if you sell at a loss, you get a tax deduction) and put the cash into an IRA or Keogh (for another deduction). Once under the umbrella of the IRA or Keogh, you could even use the cash to buy stock in GM.

Where can you invest your Keogh or IRA money? Just about anywhere, as long as some institution acts as trustee. The best place to go first is any bank. Most can provide brochures and answer your questions. Other institutions eager to enroll you in Keogh or IRA retirement plans are credit unions, mutual funds, life insurance companies, and brokerage firms. You can even arrange with a brokerage firm to set up a trusteed account which you yourself manage, selecting whichever securities you wish (including zero-coupon bonds—see chapter 3), and selling them to buy others whenever you like.

You can, moreover, have plans with more than one trustee. You may have some money in a savings bank, other money in a brokerage account, and still other money in a mutual fund. And you may transfer money from one trustee to another—just so long as you never take it out of trusteeship for your own uses along the way. (Actually, with an IRA, but not a Keogh, you may take possession of the cash for 60 days. But it's easier—and safer—simply to direct the first custodian to liquidate your account and transfer the funds directly to the second. Both will be old hands at this and will send you the necessary forms.) Some mutual fund "families" allow you to switch from one to another of their group of funds at will, without changing trustees or incurring special charges.

The most obvious place *not* to invest Keogh or IRA money is in municipal bonds. Why accept their low tax-free yields when anything you put into your retirement fund will grow tax-free anyway? Similarly, because the money grows tax-free and is all taxed as income when it is withdrawn, *dividends and interest are just as valuable as long-term capital gains*—even though ordinarily $1 of long-term capital gains is worth more, after taxes, than $1 of dividends. So there is even more reason than usual to adhere to the bird-in-the-hand philosophy of investing, rather than forgoing current dividends or interest in the hope of realizing large capital gains.

Retirement accounts are *not* places to take much risk. Losses within one of these plans aren't tax-deductible. And every $1,000 lost in the early years means an ultimate loss of the tens of thousands it might have grown to. For many people, the best place to start is at a bank, credit union, or savings and loan. These are safe, convenient, and inexpensive: most charge no custodial fee. Later, when your fund has grown more substantial, you might well wish to transfer part or all of it someplace more sophisticated.

Beyond that, the question of how to invest your retirement money is really the subject of this whole book, not just one or two paragraphs. I began my own Keogh plan at a savings bank. Now it is invested in stocks and bonds.

What forms do you fill out? Whichever institution(s) you grace with your business will help you with the red tape. Basically, there is little. Nor do you even have to file special tax forms each year as you once did. Just enter your IRA and Keogh contributions each year as indicated on form 1040. And note this: These contributions will lower your "taxable income," and hence your taxes, *whether you itemize deductions or not*.

What does the trustee charge? It varies from nothing, at most savings banks, to quite a lot at some brokerage firms. Be sure to find out in advance. Where stocks and bonds are involved, there will be both brokerage commissions, for buying and selling, *and* a fee for the trustee (often an obscure savings bank with which the brokerage firm has affiliated for the purpose of offering these plans). With life insurance companies, there are likely to be all kinds of extra costs, both explicit and hidden. Watch out! Ordinarily, I would avoid setting up an insurance-company-trusteed plan.

What is an IRA "rollover" account? This is for people who leave jobs where they have been accruing tax-sheltered pension benefits already. Upon leaving, they are likely to be paid at least some portion of those accrued benefits in a lump sum—which then exposes them to income tax. However, if you act within 60 days, you may put the entire sum, however large, into an IRA rollover account and avoid exposing it to taxation.

What is a Salary Reduction Plan? Increasingly popular, these plans are set up by employers. If your employer has one (they are also known as "401K" plans), you're in luck. You will be allowed to lop off a portion of your salary, typically 5 to 15%, with that money being sent straight to a tax-sheltered retirement account managed for your benefit. As with an IRA, the money you set aside for retirement is shielded from income tax. *But the Salary Reduction Plan has four additional advantages:* First, your contributions will be shielded from Social Security tax as well (although that could lower your eventual Social Security benefits). Second, there is no $2,000 ceiling on annual contributions. Third, withdrawals qualify for 10-year forward income averaging. Under this provision (which applies, as well, to Keogh Plans), the tax on withdrawals after age 59½ can be greatly minimized. Fourth, early withdrawals are permitted without penalty, so long as the purpose of the withdrawal is to "stave off hardship." (Whatever that means. It remains to be seen whether the lack of an above-ground swimming pool will, in the eyes of the IRS, constitute hardship.)

If you are offered such a plan, you should probably sign up. And if you have still more money you'd like to sock away free of taxes, you can contribute to an IRA as well. You can have both.

Can you borrow against the value of your fund? Not in the sense of putting it up as collateral. This is strictly forbidden. However, if when you go for a personal loan it is evident that you have tens or hundreds of thousands of dollars saved up in a retirement plan—which you could draw on, with penalties, if you had to—it could help you get the loan.

When can you begin withdrawing your money? To avoid penalty you must wait until you are at least 59½. Between ages 59½ and 70½ you may withdraw as little or as much as you want. From 70½ on, you must withdraw certain minimums each year, keyed to your life expectancy. Failure to do so triggers a whopping penalty.

Must you be retired? No. At least not as far as the IRS is concerned. However, a few Keogh Plan trustees do make this a provision of their plan, so find out in advance.

How is the money withdrawn? Your funds may be withdrawn all at once, or over a period of years that is keyed to your life expectancy (or the combined life expectancy of you and your spouse). Choosing the latter method allows the balance to continue to compound tax-free. With a Keogh Plan (but not an IRA), if you do withdraw the money all at once, it is taxed, mercifully, under special "ten-year forward" income-averaging regulations that greatly reduce the bite. (To qualify for these special regulations, you must have been a participant in a Keogh Plan for at least the previous five years.)

What if you die or become disabled? Upon death or permanent total disability—regardless of your age—the entire fund may be withdrawn without penalty, either all at once or over a period of years. If you die, the beneficiary named in your plan has the option of rolling over the proceeds of the fund into an IRA of his or her own.

What if you have employees? If you set up a Keogh Plan for yourself you are required to make contributions for your employees' retirements as well. However, you can set up the plan in such a way that your employees do not become eligible to participate until they have been working for you for three years.

What if you have partners? If your income is derived from a partnership, there are further regulations—ask your accountant.

What if you are already over 59½? It's not too late to set up one of these retirement plans—and the tax savings can still be substantial.

Further questions? Write the nearest Internal Revenue Service office for IRS publication 590 and struggle through it, or ask the retirement expert at your savings bank, or your accountant, to help you.

Retirement plans are not a way to grow rich slowly, let alone quick. If interest rates *do* stay high (or go even higher), it will only be because inflation simultaneously eats steadily away at purchasing power. Thus $1 million in 30 or 40 years may well be like $100,000 now—a lot, but not "rich." If interest rates decline, you will be locked into high rates on what you contribute now (if you choose long-term bonds or stocks whose dividends are maintained or increased)—but you won't be able to reinvest the income those contributions generate at the same high rates, and so may not have $1 million after all.

Neither way will you be "rich." But either way you could well be comfortable, and that's very nearly as good.

Part Two

The Stock Market

CHAPTER 5

Meanwhile, Down at the Track

October. This is one of the peculiarly dangerous months to
speculate in stocks. Others are November, December,
January, February, March, April, May, June, July, August,
and September.

—Mark Twain

OK. You have some money in a savings bank; you have
set up an Individual Retirement Account—and a Keogh
Plan, if possible—and are contributing to them at the
maximum rate allowed; you have equity in a home, if you
want it; you've tied up $1,000 in bulk purchases of tunafish
and shaving cream; you have lowered your auto and
homeowner's insurance premiums by increasing your
deductibles; you have adequate term life insurance;
you've paid off all your 18% installment loans; there is a
little solar water heater sitting on your roof above your
well-insulated attic; and you own enough IBM (or some
other solid common, or even preferred, stock) to take full
advantage of the $100 ($200) dividend tax exclusion. In
short, you have done all the things that scream to be done.
You have made the easy decisions.

Now what?

There are three compelling reasons to invest a portion of
your funds in stocks.

1. *Over the long run—and it may be very long—stocks
should outperform bonds*. The reason is that stock and
bond prices are set in the open market—and the market,
over the long run, rewards risk. From 1926 to 1975, the
total compounded annual rate of return you would have
had from buying risk-free United States Treasury bills was
2.3%; the return from slightly riskier corporate bonds would

have been 3.8%, and the return from stocks would have been 9%. The compounded annual rate of inflation during the same period was 2.3%. Ignoring taxes, $1,000 invested in corporate bonds over that time span would have grown to $6,200, but to $68,200 if invested in stocks.

In the eight years from 1975 through the end of 1982, inflation galloped along at an 8.3% compounded rate and the return you would have earned from Treasury bills—before tax—kept pace. Stocks, when you include their dividends (again before taxes), compounded almost twice as fast.

Of course, you can play with numbers like these, depending on the time periods you choose. There were some pretty dreadful five- and ten-year stretches nestled in among those 57 years (in case you hadn't noticed), during which you would have been much better off in bonds or even a savings account. Timing is very important. Granted, too, the ability of equity (stocks) to outperform debt (bonds) —and to beat inflation—has had much to do with America's more or less steadily improving productivity, which may or may not improve as rapidly in the future. The world has changed. Resources are scarcer; foreign competition is stronger; businesses are more highly regulated, even if that trend may have peaked; confidence in the future, and hence investment, is not what it once was; inflation lurks; and, because of inflation, bond rates are a great deal higher than that 3.8% fifty-year average. Yet the fact remains that over the long run, because the market *knows* all these things, stocks will be priced low enough to offer buyers reason to buy.

(And it just might be that we have been going through a sort of toughening-up process over the last several years, and that our sensational technological prowess has been paving the way for enormous strides forward.)

2. *Unlike bonds, stocks offer at least the potential of keeping up with inflation,* even if that potential is by no means always realized. Once the interest rate on a bond is set, it's set. Bread could go to $2 a loaf, and the bond

wouldn't pay a nickel more in interest. But ITT, which owns the company that bakes the bread, might—might—be able to keep its profits, and its dividend, rising in step with inflation.

3. *If all goes well, stocks can act as a tax shelter*. Long-term capital gains are taxed only 40% as heavily as ordinary income. But more than that, by choosing a stock that pays out little or none of its profits in dividends, you pay little or no tax on your share of those profits. Instead, the company retains and reinvests them for you. If they do so profitably—in a great new product or a more efficient factory, say—future profits, and your share of them, will be even larger. This is the bird-in-the-bush strategy of investing. One of its drawbacks derives from the fact that corporate accounting, even when practiced with pure motives, is a matter of judgment, at best. The only profit statement you can truly bank on is a dividend check that doesn't bounce.

Nonetheless, with this bird-in-the-bush strategy you can ultimately profit two ways. First, after a period of years the company you've invested in may decide to pay out a greater portion of its (by-then-greater) profits as dividends. You will then have to pay income tax on those dividends, but in the meantime you've been reinvesting, through the company, money the government would otherwise have taken. Second, you can sell your stock. If the company has indeed invested your profits wisely, there is a chance, but by no means a certainty, that you will get more for it than you paid—perhaps even several times as much.

It thus becomes a matter of some interest just how well a company is likely to reinvest all those profits they don't pay you as dividends. Unfortunately, there is no way to know for sure. However, you can determine how well they've done—or, because accounting is open to so much qualification and interpretation, *seem* to have done—in the past. The number you are looking for is "return on equity," and it is, simply, the company's profits expressed as a percentage of all the money shareholders have dumped in over the years, much of it by forgoing dividends.

There are companies like IBM which have been able to reinvest those accumulated unpaid dividends at returns well above 15% a year; and there are others, like B. F. Goodrich, that have earned less than half as much on the money left with them. And then there are the Braniffs, which have diddled it away altogether.

Naturally, investors would much prefer stock in companies like the former than the latter, all other things being equal. So all other things are *not* equal: You have to pay more for stock in companies that are known to reinvest profits at a high rate of return. Indeed, there was a time (1973) when you had to pay $60 or more to get a one-dollar slice of Avon's profit pie, so excited were investors by Avon's ability to earn 25 to 30% on that dollar.* At the same time it cost only $8 to buy a $1 slice of Goodrich's profit pie. What investors failed to note was that, while 25% was a boffo return on that one reinvested Avon dollar, $1—no matter how well it was reinvested—was a pretty lousy return on a $60 investment! Subsequently Avon stock fell about 85% even though profits kept growing admirably, and as I write this you have to pay only $10 for a one-dollar slice of Avon's ever-growing profit pie. (Thirty dollars a share, each of which earned nearly $3 in the preceding 12 months.) One reason for this is that the ever-growing profit pie shrank in 1980, 1981, and 1982.

So there's more to choosing the right stock than finding the company with the highest "return on equity." But I'm getting ahead of myself. I should not talk like this until you know as much about the essentials of the stock market—the forest—as the professionals do. This will take up most of the rest of the chapter. (Getting to know as much about the trees could take up most of the rest of your life.)

---

* Avon was earning a little over $2 in profit for each of its shares. The shares went for $140 apiece.

The stock market could hardly be simpler. There are just two ways a stock can go: up or down. There are just two emotions that tug in those opposite directions: greed and fear. There are just two ways to make money on a stock: dividends and capital gains. And there are just two kinds of investors in the market: the "public," like you or me; and the "institutions," like bank trust departments and mutual funds and insurance companies. It's the amateurs against the professionals, and it's not at all clear who has the advantage. Often, both lose. Finally—and here it gets only slightly more complicated—there are just three kinds of stocks:

1. There are 300 or 400 stocks that the institutions keep tabs on and in which they eagerly invest. These command premium prices, although hardly the way they once did, in the early seventies, when Avon was selling for 60 times its profits. You should be wary of these stocks, as they can hardly represent "overlooked value."

2. There are perhaps another 300 or 400 stocks the institutions follow but do not invest in with any enthusiasm. They are out of fashion, and thus at least worth considering. Some day they could return to fashion.

3. And then there are the great majority of stocks that the institutions neither follow nor invest in but simply ignore. These are called the bottom-tier stocks, because they have been relegated to the pits. Some of them, under certain circumstances, may be worth your money.

All stocks fall into another three categories as well. They are all either overvalued, fairly valued, or undervalued.

To suggest any correlation between these two sets of categories—to suggest, that is, that institutional favorites are overvalued, middle-tier stocks fairly valued, and bottom-tier stocks undervalued—would, of course, be the height of oversimplification, not to mention financial heresy. Still, it's a thought to keep in mind.

What is a stock worth? Market veterans will tell you that a stock is worth whatever people are willing to pay for it.

Price is determined by supply and demand. If lots of people want it, it will be worth a lot. If everyone ignores it, it won't be worth spitting at.

But it is too simple to say that a stock is worth whatever people will pay for it, because what people are willing to pay for it depends, in turn, on what they think it is worth. It is a circular definition, used as a rationalization of financial foolishness rather than as a rational way to appraise value.

The value of a stock should not be nearly so subjective as, say, the value of a Picasso sketch or a 1909S VDB penny. Rather than entitling its owner to some inestimable esthetic pleasure or some irreplaceable rarity, a share of stock merely entitles the owner to a share of present and future profits (or, in the event of bankruptcy or acquisition by another company, assets). Where two paintings of equal size may reasonably command vastly different values, two companies of equal profits, assets, and prospects should not. Yet they do.

The market veteran will readily agree that this is irrational, but he will ask you, with a laugh, "Who ever said the stock market was rational?"

That gets the market veteran off the hook and may eliminate in his mind the need to search for value. But there are other market veterans, perhaps even a majority by now, who believe that over the long run rationality does pay off in the market. Sooner or later, they say, bubbles burst; sooner or later, bargains are recognized. A company cannot prosper forever without its shareholders at some point benefiting.

Indeed, if the market is driven by irrational greed and fear to excesses of over- and undervaluation, as it surely is, then it is the rational man, they say, seeing these excesses for what they are, who will be buying the excessively undervalued stock, particularly when the market as a whole is depressed; and selling the excessively overvalued stock, particularly when the market as a whole is on high ground. Thus may he profit from the swings in between.

All of this assumes that a rational man can determine what a stock is "really" worth.

Rational men differ. A company's future prospects—and even its current profits—are open to widely differing assessments. Obviously, no one can answer precisely what a stock is worth. But that doesn't eliminate the need to arrive at some rational valuation, or the possibility of setting some reasonable guidelines for doing so.

What a stock is worth depends at any given time on the alternative investments that are then available. It is a question of relative value. Think of investments as wallets. A 5% savings account is a wallet you can buy for $20 that miraculously fills up with $1 (5%) by the end of every year. It is safe and convenient—you can "sell" it whenever you want and be sure of getting back your full $20—but it's not a great investment. At the time of this writing you can buy other "wallets" that fill up with the same $1 just as fast—not for $20 but for a mere $10. Namely, high-grade bonds that pay 10% interest.

You can say the first wallet sells for "20 times earnings" and the second for "10 times earnings." This is the famous "price/earnings ratio," or "multiple," you have heard so much about, although it's generally applied to stocks, not bonds or wallets.*

Now. If a virtually risk-free investment like an IBM bond sells for 10 times earnings, what should a stock sell for?

On the one hand, a stock should sell for *less*, because it involves more risk. There is no guarantee that the $1 will show up in the wallet by the end of the year—or even that the wallet itself will be in any shape for you to sell it to someone else, should you so desire. What's more, only a portion of your $1 is actually paid out to you as a cash

---

* You will find "p/e ratios" listed, along with dividends and prices, in the stock pages of most newspapers.

dividend. Much, most, or all of it may be retained by the company.

On the other hand, a stock should perhaps sell for *more*, because it involves more potential reward (either the earnings or stock price could go *up*) and because of the tax advantages referred to earlier.

In deciding how much more or less to pay for a stock than the 10 times earnings you might pay for a savings certificate or high-grade bond—or whatever the going rate is at the time you read this—one weighs the extra risk against the potential for extra return.

For stock in a moribund company whose earnings seem likely to decline each year right into bankruptcy, you would not pay very much no matter how good past earnings have been.

For stock in a company whose earnings over the long run seem about as likely to increase as to decrease—where risk and reward about cancel one another out—you might expect to pay 10 times earnings. So if you find such a stock selling for 5 or 6 times earnings—as many do—it could look pretty good.

For stock in a company whose earnings seem likely to be able to keep pace with inflation—no "real" growth, that is, but growth in earnings all the same—you might expect to pay more than the 10 times earnings you would pay for a high-grade bond, the earnings of which do not rise with inflation. In fact, companies like this have also sold recently at 5 or 6 times earnings. A bargain? You bet.

Finally, for stock in a company whose prospects are really bright, with the possibility of real growth of 5% or 10% or even 20% a year for the foreseeable future, you might expect to pay a lot more than 10 times earnings—as the banks did with Avon. One serious problem, however, is that the future has consistently proved remarkably unforeseeable. There are always loads of well-reasoned and seemingly conservative projections around; but the funniest things happen on the way to the future.

All other things being equal—that is, if *all* stocks were

selling at 10 times earnings—you would choose only those companies whose earnings were expected to grow the fastest. But the question is not whether a fast-growing company is better than a slow-growing one. Any idiot knows that IBM is a better *company* than Suave Shoe. The question is whether you should pay 15 times earnings for the one or 5 to 6 times earnings for the other. Which stock, at any given time, is a better *relative value*? The real trick—and payoff—is to find a company selling for 6 times earnings that you think will grow as fast as the one selling for 15 times earnings. Then you know for sure which one to buy.*

Admittedly, it's not quite this simple. For one thing, it makes sense to look not just at what a company may earn, but also at what it *owns*. A company whose business is lousy, but which happens to be conducted on 50,000 acres of wholly owned real estate between Dallas and Fort Worth, might have a liquidation value—if you closed down the business and paid off all the creditors—of $25 a share. Yet such land might be valued on the company's books at next to nothing, if it had been acquired earlier in the century—so it might not even show up in quick calculations of the company's "book value." It could be what's known as a hidden asset, and well worth buying shares in, regardless of the company's dismal earnings.

I should also stress that the 10 times earnings I've been using as a benchmark is by no means eternal. It all depends on what wallets are going for at any given time. If you can get 15% from a high-grade 20-year corporate bond—or by paying off the balance of your 15% 20-year mortgage, for that matter, which amounts to much the same thing—then you have a low-risk wallet that produces $1 for every $6.67 you put up—6.7 times earnings. The

---

* When I wrote this in 1977, IBM was selling around $65 a share (15 times earnings), and the stock I compared it with, U.S. Shoe—not Suave Shoe—was selling at $15 (6 times earnings). Six years later, IBM stock is up 50%, but U.S. Shoe has tripled (and then some). Like IBM's, its earnings grew; unlike IBM's, so did its multiple—from 6 times earnings to 11 times. The pros have begun to like it. So I've had to substitute a different boring shoe company to make the example work.

higher the prevailing interest rate on savings certificates or
high-grade corporate bonds—or mortgage prepayments—the
less you should be willing to pay for stocks. And vice
versa.

Now it happens that far from looking at assets or relative value, the professional money managers of the late
sixties and early seventies—particularly those at the banks,
which manage tens of billions of dollars of other people's
money—concentrated their attention and their megabucks
on a relative handful of fast-growing companies, bidding
their prices up to truly remarkable heights. The "nifty
fifty," these stocks were called—"glamour" stocks, "one-
decision" stocks (you just had to decide to buy them; you
would never sell them, no matter what price you could
get). The group included such indisputably fine companies
as Polaroid, Disney, Avon, IBM, Coca-Cola, Kodak, Xerox,
and McDonald's.

Most stocks they ignored altogether. Not because they
lacked merit—although, admittedly, some of them did—
but because it's a lot less trouble to put $100 million into
Johnson & Johnson than to stay late at the office each
night hunting for 50 less visible companies—perhaps better values—in which to invest $2 million each. The first
rule of fiduciary bureaucracy was (and is): You can't be
criticized for losing money in IBM. Corollary: He who
does what everyone else does will not do appreciably
worse. In other words, it was *unfortunate* to lose money in
IBM, Avon, Polaroid, or Xerox; but it would have been
imprudent to lose somewhat less money in the stocks of
companies no one ever heard of.

In talking with people who managed billions of dollars
at some of the nation's largest banks during this period, I
got the distinct impression that it would have been
undignified for top-drawer financial institutions like theirs
to invest in anything but large, top-drawer American
corporations.

That posture has a fiduciary ring to it, until you consider
how much extra the banks were paying to invest in such

firms, and how much they ultimately lost for their clients by doing so.

One money manager from a major New York bank told me that it was his bank's policy to invest only in companies whose earnings they expected to grow at an above-average rate. What about companies they expected to grow at only an average or subaverage rate? No, he said, they did not buy stock in such companies. Regardless of price? Regardless of price. Was there *any* price at which the bank would buy stock in an average-growth company?

This question made the money manager uncomfortable. He clearly wanted to answer no, because he clearly would be damned before he would buy stock in such a company. But he couldn't come right out and say that, because he knew that, theoretically, there must be *some* price at which he should choose the stock of the mediocre company over the stocks of his nifty fifty.

It's not that the bank had compared some of the low-multiple stocks with some of the high-multiple stocks and decided consciously that, yes, the high-multiple stocks represented a better value despite their premium prices. Rather, the policy (dogma?) was based on studies that showed how, over the long run, the best way to beat the stock market averages had been to buy stock in companies whose earnings grew faster than average. That's how things had worked in the past, and that's why 51% of this bank's discretionary billions were invested in just 14 stocks, only one of which, at the time of our luncheon, was selling for less than 20 times earnings.

At one point in this madness, in fact, a few years ago, you had a great many of the nation's otherwise intelligent, well-educated, exceptionally well-bred and well-paid fiduciaries valuing the Avon Corporation more highly than the Ford Motor Company and Gulf + Western Industries *combined*. This despite the fact that Ford and Gulf + Western had $25 billion in sales to Avon's $1 billion; $15 billion in assets to Avon's $700 million; and $1 billion in profits to Avon's $135 million. Not only that, Ford and

Gulf + Western were paying out $280 million a year in dividends that year, compared with $85 million for Avon.

It was true that if Avon continued to grow at its then-average 14% a year, and if Ford and Gulf + Western grew more slowly, Avon's profits would have grown to equal the combined profits of the other two in a mere 25 years or so (although in the meantime it would have paid out much less in dividends). But why wait 25 years for profits which, for the same money, the money managers could have owned then and there?

Since then, Avon and stocks like it have fallen sharply in price, while Ford and Gulf + Western and others like them—for all the rough sledding of recent years—have done much better. But what's important is not that you should have shorted Avon back then and bought Ford and Gulf + Western (although you would indeed have made a killing); what's important is that this sort of irrational imbalance could have occurred at all.

On Wall Street it happens all the time, if not always on such a grand scale. And herein, I suggest, may lie an opportunity.

Even though the major institutions, which account for two-thirds or more of the trading in stocks, have of late been searching much more widely for good values, there are still a great many companies that are largely or entirely ignored—*whether they are exceptional values or not.*

Subject to the caveats and additional suggestions in the next chapters, here is what for most people has to be about the most sensible way to invest in stocks, if they are going to invest in stocks at all:

1. To begin with, only invest money you won't have to touch, if need be, for many years. Retirement is not a great time to start buying stocks. People who buy stocks when they get bonuses and sell them when the roof starts to leak are entrusting their investment decision to their roofs.

2. Buy low and sell high. You laugh. Yet even though this is quite obviously the key to success, most people, particularly small investors, shun the market when it is getting drubbed and venture back only after it has recovered and appears, once again, to be "healthy." *It is precisely when the market looks worst that the opportunities are best; precisely when things are good again that the opportunities are slimmest and the risks greatest.*

Item: At what was probably the most opportune time to buy stocks since the Great Depression, December of 1974, with the Dow Jones industrial average struggling to break above 600 and countless lesser stocks selling for a half or a third or even a quarter of their book values, financial columnist Eliot Janeway was advising small investors to stay away. "No investment market in the coming year," he said with his customary self-assurance, "is going to be safe for civilians." In point of fact, the Dow climbed 40% in 1975, and many of the stocks that had been battered far worse than the Dow "blue chips" doubled and tripled.

Item: A Washington D.C., investment club purchased 200 shares of stock at 18. "Club sold all holdings at 12½," it reported to *Black Enterprise* magazine, *"due to decline in price;* intends to reinvest *when price moves up."* (Italics mine.) What kind of strategy is *that*?"

Torn as we all are between greed and fear, we tend to do just the wrong thing. When the economy is sinking fast and stocks faster, we get more and more scared. Finally, we quit in disgust. Better to get out with a big loss, we say to ourselves, than to watch our holdings disappear altogether. In fact, of course, this is just the time to be getting into the market, not out.

By the same token, avoid investing when the market is generally judged to be healthy, when you are becoming excited by the gains in some of the stocks you already own, when prospects for the economy are generally conceded to be bright, and when people are talking about the real possibility that the Dow Jones industrial average will finally break through to new ground. *In such a climate people are expect-*

ing good news. If it comes, it won't move the market much because it has been so widely anticipated. If, by chance, bad news should come instead, that will move the market—down.

Whether concerning an individual stock, or the market as a whole, always ask yourself which would be more of a surprise: good news or bad news. News that is expected never has as much impact—if any at all—as news that is not.

"The truth is," market analyst Dr. Martin Zweig has written,

that the stock market does best when earnings and dividends are getting drubbed, and worst when [they] are zooming. For example: In the fourth quarter of 1972 and the first quarter of 1973 . . . earnings of the Dow Industrials soared upward by 35% over year-earlier periods. The market responded by crashing more violently than at any time since the 'thirties. Then, amid the depths of pessimism, first- and second-quarter 1975 Dow profits collapsed an average of 31%; yet the stock market simultaneously vaulted 43%, one of the best six-month surges in history.

Another of the very best six-month surges was the explosion that began in August 1982. Unemployment was higher than at any time since the Depression, business leaders had finally lost confidence in Reagan, the international banks were widely believed to be all but officially bankrupt, the federal deficit was projected soon to exceed the total output of all but a few of the world's industrialized nations, and (on the lighter side) Joe Granville was screaming that the worst was yet to come. And the market soared.

It works the same way, only in reverse, when the market is peaking.

"One reason that so many investors get overloaded with stocks at market tops," Zweig continues,

is their ill-founded reasoning: "Business looks good." It *always* looks good at the peaks. With prospects ripe for continued gains in earnings and dividends, investors optimistically lick their chops in anticipation of further market appreciation. But something goes astray. Business gets too overheated; the scramble for borrowed money to keep the boom rolling grows more intense, pressuring interest rates upward. The Federal Reserve, spotting increasing inflation, begins to tighten monetary growth, further exacerbating the surge in interest rates. Then, as short-term money instruments such as Treasury bills become more yield-attractive, the stock market begins to groan as the switching away from stocks accelerates, aided in no small part by the illiquidity in overly optimistic investors' portfolios [investors, that is, who have spent all their money on stocks already, and now have no more cash with which to buy any more]. Yet, most folks just continue holding their stocks—or worse, buying more—because "Business looks good." Finally, many months later it becomes apparent that business has slowed down . . . but it's too late for most investors. They've already been trapped by a crumbling stock market. "Optimism" gives way to "hope" that the business slowdown won't become a recession. But the drop in stock prices rocks consumer confidence, business dips some more and recession is reality. The stock market slump becomes a rout and investors' "hopes" are finally dashed. Seeing that a recession is in progress, investors "know" that earnings will slump; in "panic" they sell their stock, absorbing huge losses. Finally, all that selling, amid tons of pessimism, improves stock market liquidity [people once again have some cash], building a base for a new boom in the market, . . . one which *always* begins before business turns up.*

That's the cycle, all right, but it is easier to identify in hindsight than on any given Tuesday morning when you are trying to figure out which way business, and stocks, are headed. If in the early sixties you had held off investing while you waited for the next recession, you would have had to sit on the sidelines for six or eight years. "Business looked good"—and *was* good—for nearly a decade.

So for most people, the most practical, prudent alternative to trying to spot market tops and bottoms is to:

3. Diversify over time by not investing all at once.
Spread your investments out to smooth the peaks and valleys of the market. Only, skip investing when the stock market averages are making new highs (or approaching old ones),

---

* *The Zweig Forecast*, 747 Third Ave., New York, NY 10017.

and invest extraheavily in periods when the averages are making new lows (or approaching old ones). The best times to invest are when the market has just taken a terrible dive of several days' or weeks' duration, and when talk of depression, the new bear market, and/or nuclear holocaust is rife. If the depression does come (and usually it does not), at least you will have been prudent enough to invest only money you didn't need to touch for years (Rule #1). And in the event of the holocaust, it wouldn't make much difference.

By investing more when the market is low and less when it is high, you will come out ahead when it is somewhere in between.

4. Diversify over several stocks in different industries. If all your money is riding on two or three stocks, you are exposed to much more risk than if you have diversified over a dozen or more. And, as stocks of companies within the same industry tend to move together, you will only be truly diversified if you choose from among different sectors of the economy.

5. And "diversify" in the same stock, by what's known as dollar-cost-averaging. To wit: If you are planning to buy 300 shares of a stock at $14, consider buying only 100 instead. Then if the stock never goes down and you never buy more, you can hardly complain. But if the natural ups and downs of life make the stock available some time later at, say, $12, you might then buy 100 or 200 shares more. It will be that much better a value.

Part of the theory here is that if you are in a terrible rush to buy the 300 shares, convinced that the stock is about to take off and there's not a minute to lose—you are very likely reacting to some hot news. And believe me, unless you are an insider trading (illegally) on privileged information, chances are you are one of the last to hear this hot news. Nine times out of ten you will be buying your shares from someone who heard it first. In which case, when the dust settles you may not regret having snagged only 100 shares instead of 300. If, on the other hand, you are not reacting to any particular news when you decide to purchase the stock, it is simply unlikely that the stock would go straight up without any dips from the day you buy it. And dips allow you to average down your cost.

Attracted by its 9% yield and hopelessly ignorant of its problems, I once bought 50 shares of Con Edison, Rock of Gibraltar, at 20. Shortly thereafter Con Ed omitted its quarterly dividend for the first time in twelve thousand years and, to my dismay, I found myself buying 100 more shares at 12. Then 100 more at 8½. Then, even, 100 more at 6. I kept buying because I just could not believe that the State of New York—which needed only to grant Con Ed's rate requests to solve all its problems—would prefer to have the company go bankrupt, and thus have to take on the burden of power generation itself. (Especially considering New York's own financial position at the time.) Sure enough, the state began cooperating, the dividend gradually was restored (even raised a notch), and the stock recovered to 20. (It would later go on to double and split.) I would be lying if I told you I was smart enough to hold all 350 shares, or even most of them, all the way back up to 20. Dumb! But at least I held some. And I made sure that the first 50 shares I sold were the 50 I had purchased at 20, thus giving me a nice short-term capital loss to help out with my taxes. The last shares I sold I had held long enough to qualify for a long-term capital gain.

Strictly speaking, dollar-cost-averaging is a little fancier than what I've described here. Strictly speaking, the idea is to invest in a stock, or in the market, in equal dollar amounts on a regular basis—say, $3,000 mailed to a mutual fund faithfully at the end of each year. By doing so, you will buy more shares when the fund is low and fewer when it is high. And look what happens. Say the price of shares in the Sakoff Illustration Fund (and hence the number you can buy) fluctuates as follows: $25 (120 shares), $45 (67), $25 (120), $5 (600), $25 (120). The shares went up $20, came home, went down $20, and came home again. (This is, remember, the Sakoff Illustration Fund.)

Yet even though shares are no higher than when you started—$25—and even though they went down as much as they went up and averaged $25 for all five periods, do you think you only wind up with the $15,000 you put in? No, you wind up with—Ta-Da!—$25,675. That's dollar-cost-averaging. It forces you to buy more shares when they're low, fewer when they're high.

★ **6. A program of periodic investments in no-load mutual funds** is for many people the most practical way to achieve diversification—let alone to avoid worrying about all this in the first place. (See chapter 8.) However, if you *are* choosing your own stocks:

7. Be wary of high-multiple stocks, even though they are the stocks of outstanding companies—and stocks which may, in the fullness of time, do extremely well. Their hefty multiples (price/earnings ratios) discount earnings growth far into the future. Which is to say that even if the growth comes in on schedule, the stocks may not go up. They're *already* up. And for most of us, it is hard to see that far into the future anyway. Should earnings not continue to grow as expected, such stocks can collapse, even though the underlying company may remain sound. What's more, it can hardly be argued that these stocks have been ignored and that they therefore represent some hidden value Wall Street had failed to discover.

8. Don't buy, stocks that "everyone" is recommending, regardless of the multiples at which they sell.

A few years back I attended an *Institutional Investor* conference—1,000 money managers representing billions upon billions of dollars. The men who really move the market. One of the panel sessions was devoted exclusively to ITT. The seminar organizer hadn't been able to find anyone bearish on the stock, so three of the panelists were bullish and the fourth volunteered to play devil's advocate.

Well, when I heard their discussion, and saw all the heads nodding in the audience—at 1,000 shares a nod, I figured—I got this very guilty rush of adrenaline. What if I ran out of the room, rushed to the pay phone, and bought ITT? Would that be misuse of inside information? I decided it would not, and that's exactly what I did. At $44 a share. Any fool could see that at least a *few* of these men would do much the same thing after the meeting, or certainly when they got back to their desks. If they were not interested in ITT stock, why were they sitting through this seminar? And as there was no opposition meeting going on that I knew of persuading an equal number of people to rush to the phones and sell, I figured there would just have to be buying pressure on the stock. How could I miss?

The stock went straight down to 12.

Apparently, they had all put ITT in their portfolios and were now waiting for it to go up. But there was no one left to buy it. (I got out at 34 on the way down. What I *should* have done was buy the stock at 12, because it has since recovered.)

9. Choose instead bottom-tier stocks. Bottom-tier stocks can't fall out of favor—they are already out of favor.

10. Choose mostly stocks that pay attractive dividends. These stocks will, necessarily, be selling at low price/earnings ratios. They should be selling so low, and yielding such attractive dividends, not because they are in declining industries or because they have serious long-term problems (as some are and do), but simply because they have been ignored.

You can never know for sure, of course, that a dividend won't be lowered or omitted, but you will be safest with companies that have been in business and paying dividends for many years; companies that have weathered a recession or two without cutting their dividend; companies whose earnings have generally been improving from year to year; companies with relatively little long-term debt; and companies whose dividends, although high, represent a relatively small portion of cash flow* in a typical year. A company that

---

*A company's cash flow is its profits *plus* those expenditures it doesn't really expend, like depreciation, *minus* capital expenditures (which must be paid for with cash, but are not charged against profits). One handy place to find cash flow information is Value Line—see page 99.

earns $1 a share and pays out 90 cents has much less room to maneuver than one that pays out 90 cents but earns $2.

If you cannot find such stocks, the market is probably too high. Stay away! Don't buy stocks just because you have money to burn, or because friends you know are talking about their profits. Wait.

The companies you choose may be in lackluster industries; or they may be in the midst of serious short-term *but temporary and surmountable* problems. When the problem first loomed, typically, "smart money" bailed out. Accordingly, the stock dropped sharply, then drifted lower for months as it became conventional wisdom not to buy such a dog—even though the price was now much lower and the problem, whatever it was, well on the way to solution.

Morse Shoe (yet another boring shoe company) once sold as high as 25, when Wall Street was happy to pay 15 or 20 times earnings for a fine little growth company. Its earnings from 1964 to 1969 had been 60 cents a share, 84 cents, $1.10, $1.20, $1.41, $1.56. A great trend-line.

Luckily I had never heard of Morse Shoe back then (although I had, sadly, heard of several others). The stock market turned sour, the longest business expansion in recent history came to an end, inflation began eating away at the country and raising interest rates and lowering bond and stock prices—and to top it all off, Morse Shoe's earnings began going in the wrong direction. The company operated leased shoe departments in chain stores around the country, and some of those chains, preferring to run the departments themselves, were giving Morse Shoe the boot.

I saw Morse Shoe for the first time, in 1973, in a list of stocks *Forbes* considered undervalued. The stock was around 1, down from 25, and earnings had dipped to 23 cents a share. According to *Forbes*, the company had a book value—the things it owned less the things it owed—of around $8 a share.

The stock was out of favor. What self-respecting institutional money manager was going to buy a stock, even for $1, whose earnings since 1969 had gone steadily down from $1.56 to 23 cents? What institution was even going to look at such a stock? Many retail brokerage houses, for their part, had arbitrary rules forbidding their reps to recommend—and in some cases even take orders for—stocks selling under $3 a share.

Yet the management of this company seemed sound, and was busily replacing lost outlets with new ones. People will probably always need shoes. In any case, the company had a net worth per share—things like cash and inventory—far in excess of its stock price. It even paid a 10-cent dividend (down from 40 cents), which on a $1 stock represented a 10% return. Still, few people would buy it. Who cared about Morse Shoe at 1 when the world was about to end? Who cared about Morse Shoe at 1 when you could buy Disney at 110?

As it happened the world did not end, Morse Shoe's earnings rebounded to $2.09 by 1976, the dividend was raised to 40 cents, and by the time the stock got up near 12 an institution or two began considering it for its portfolio. It reached 29 in 1980 and trades today around 23.

To be sure, the market may never again present such opportunities. It was wildly oversold in those bleak days of 1974 and 1975. But even if this is an extreme case, it is an example of how profitable it can be to seek out value.

Note that throughout all this Morse Shoe was a good little *company*, despite its difficulties. But at 25 in 1968 Morse Shoe was an awful *stock* (selling at a high p/e, at more than 3 times book value, and paying a 2% dividend); while at 1 it was a terrific stock (selling at 5 times depressed earnings, less than one-sixth book value, and paying a 10% dividend).

Why invest in companies nobody's ever heard of when you can invest in General Motors, Sears, Xerox, or Kodak? Why not the best? For one thing, you pay a premium for this peace of mind. But also, the peace of mind you get is at least partly illusory. True, these companies are financially all but impregnable. But their stocks can go down almost as much as any other. General Motors was $113 a share in 1965, $29 nine years later. (Recently: $63.) Xerox sold at $172 in 1972; it had dropped to $46 five years later. (Recently: $38.)

11. Beware the deceptive p/e. The price/earnings ratio is the guide most investors use to get a quick fix on a stock. It is listed in the paper every day. The p/e tells you how much p (price) you have to pay for $1 of this wallet's e (earnings).

However, the best the newspaper can do is calculate the p/e based on that day's price and *last year's* earnings. What you are buying is the right to share in next year's and future years' earnings.

It would have done you little good to know, in 1977, that Chrysler, at 16½, was selling at just 3 times its most recent year's earnings, when the following years' earnings turned out to be massive losses. The low p/e was deceptive.

Or take the opposite case. Zayre, a billion-dollar discount chain, was once a high-flying growth company selling for $47 a share. It earned around $2 a share in 1971, 1972, and 1973. In 1974 earnings dropped in the recession to a mere 14 cents. At $5 a share, the stock was listed in the paper as selling for 36 times earnings, seemingly an outrageously high multiple. Yet "book value" was over $20 a share, and there was the hope that if the economy ever recovered, and Zayre with it, the company might return to its "normal" $2-a-share earnings level, and perhaps even continue its stalled growth. Seen in that light, $5 a share was more like 2½ than 36 times earnings.

Thus in choosing stocks it is necessary to keep the p/e figure in perspective, to take an average of the last *several* years' earnings, and to think more in terms of the future than the past. This is particularly true with companies— autos, cement, construction, paper, and many others—whose profits rise and fall in cycles.

As it turned out, Zayre earnings climbed to better than $4 a share by 1982 and its stock hit 70. (W. T. Grant, on the other hand, an even larger retailer, went bankrupt. Not all troubled companies recover.)

12. Never buy a stock you think is fairly valued. Never even buy one you think should, by rights, be selling 10 or 15% higher. Always wait for one you are convinced is selling *way beneath* its fair value. Judging by its book value it should be selling much higher; judging by its future earnings potential it should be selling much higher. But it isn't. Why pay a "fair" price for a stock—which is to say, a "full" price—when so many others sell for much less? When a stock is fairly—fully—priced, there is sizable potential for loss if something goes wrong, only moderate potential for gain if things continue to go right. If the only stocks you can find seem reasonably priced, wait. When they have fallen by 20 or 40% they will look better.

There shouldn't *be* companies selling for a fraction of their reasonable value; but, at least since the early seventies and as of this writing, there are. Lots of them. Brokers will be delighted to help you find them and to supply you with information, but you might be just as well served letting *Forbes* find them for you and saving a good portion of the brokerage fees.

Forbes, more than *Business Week* or *Fortune*, is written for the investor rather than the businessman. The editors of the magazine have always stressed a level-headed, value-oriented approach to investing. They frequently run stories on companies, or whole lists of companies, that seem to be undervalued. This doesn't mean *Forbes* is always right, by any means—or even that when they are right the stock market "agrees." But for $36 a year, you can get the services of several dozen financially sophisticated editors, writers, and columnists.

13. Don't waste money subscribing to investment letters or expensive services. The more expensive investor newsletters and computer services only make sense for investors with lots of money—if then. Besides their (admittedly tax-deductible) cost there is the problem that they are liable to tempt you into buying and scare you into selling much too often, thereby incurring much higher brokerage fees and capital gains taxes than you otherwise might. There is the added problem that half the experts, at any given time, are likely to be wrong. Indeed, there is one letter which simply analyzes the sentiment of all the others—and advises you do the opposite, on the not-unreasonable theory that when most of the services are bullish, it's time to sell, and vice versa.

You want to know my idea of real market brilliance? A well-heeled former associate editor of *Fortune*, now back in the business world, sold all his stocks in March 1977, the day before the market began a rapid 100-point slide. It was pure genius. I was green with envy and admiration.

"Peter, how did you *know*?" I asked him, making a mental note to pay better heed to his opinions in the future.

"I needed the cash to buy my apartment," he said.

You can tell a lot about most publicly traded companies just by obtaining the current issue of the Standard & Poor's monthly *Stock Guide*. Many brokers give it to their clients free.

This little booklet provides key facts about almost any company you are likely to invest in: its ticker symbol; where it's traded; how many institutions own a piece; how much they own; what business the company is in; what the stock has done over the last fifteen years or so; the price/earnings ratio; dividend yield; how long a dividend has been paid; and some sketchy balance-sheet and earnings figures. One column even gives letter grades to the quality of the company's growth and stability of its earnings and dividends.

You could spend many hours writing for past annual reports, reading footnotes, consulting your accountant, even visiting the company and testing its products—but much of what you will ever know about a company you can find out in 60 seconds with the *Stock Guide*.

In three minutes more you can read the one-page summary sheet Standard & Poor's puts out on just about every public company. Brokers happily drop these sheets in the mail, if asked, or you may be able to locate them at the library. These minianalyses, while not tremendously astute, pack in a lot of relevant information.

There is one widely read investment service that *has* been shown consistently to beat the market. The weekly *Value Line Survey,* at $365 a year, ranks 1,700 stocks from 1 to 5, with Group 1 expected to do best over the coming year and Group 5 worst. Remarkably, in most of the last 18 years the rankings have performed in almost exactly the order they were supposed to. In an up year, Group 1 stocks rose more, on average, than those in the lower groups, with Group 5 stocks rising least; in down years, Group 1 stocks, on average, fell the least. Unfortunately, after taking into consideration brokerage commissions, taxes—and the chance Value Line will not work as well in the future as it has in the past—this service is no sure way to riches. But its record is nonetheless noteworthy.

Write Arnold Bernhard & Co. (5 E. 44th St. New York, NY 10017) for more information. There is generally a $33 10-week trial offer for new subscribers, and that includes a book with a page crammed full of detailed up-to-date information on each of the 1,700 stocks in the survey.

14. However you choose them, once you have selected 10 or 15 high-yielding, low-p/e stocks—not all at once, remember, diversified over time—sit back and relax. If the stocks go down, you are still getting dividends. And over the long run, unless you have chosen companies that are fundamentally unsound, it is likely that most of the stocks will at one time or another be worth a good deal more than you paid for them. This will happen either because of nothing more than the simple ups and downs of the economy and of the stock market and of your stocks in particular; or because profits and/or the dividends have increased—if only in step with inflation; or, if you are really lucky, because one of your companies gets caught up in some new financial fad (as with an insulation company around the time of the energy conservation crunch), or becomes the target of some other company's takeover bid (which, at the rate profitable or asset-rich little companies are being taken over these days, is not farfetched).

★ **15. Invest—don't speculate.** It's one thing to take risks in low-priced stocks that you hope, over time, may work out their problems and triple in value. If you can afford the risk, it may reward you handsomely.

It's quite another to jump in and out of stocks (or options or commodities), hoping to "play the market" successfully. Every time you jump, your broker cuts down your stake. Jump once a month for a year (and to the speculator a month seems an eternity), and you have transferred half your stake to your broker. Even jumping once a year is likely to cost you about as much in commissions as you would receive in dividends.

Why it costs $100 or more to buy and then sell 200 shares of stock (what—do they do it one share at a time?) when it costs just a dime or a quarter to clear a handwritten check, or $35 to prepare an entire tax return, no one knows. But as long as it does, investors of modest means cannot afford to do anything but "buy and hold," unless they are awfully confident they know which way individual stocks, and the market as a whole, are headed. Winning some and losing some just won't do when you have to fork over 5% to the dealer for each hand.

Buy value and hold it. Don't switch in and out; don't try to outsmart the market.

16. Sell only when a stock has gone up so much that you feel it no longer represents a good value. Don't sell because you think business or the market generally is going to get bad, because

• if you think so, chances are lots of other people think

so, too, and the market may already have discounted this possibility (that is, the stock price may already reflect it);

• you could be wrong;

• even if business does get bad, someday it will get better—and in the meantime you are collecting dividends rather than paying brokerage commissions and capital gains taxes.

There are one drawback and three basic risks in following the strategy of buying a preponderance of high-yielding low-p/e stocks outlined above.

The drawback: For people in high tax brackets who can't invest through a tax-deferred retirement plan of some sort, half or more of dividends go straight to the government. Such individuals may reasonably decide to disregard dividends and seek low-p/e stocks that reinvest most or all their earnings, thus deferring taxes and adding to the potential for capital gains.*

Risk number 1: Your choice of stocks will be so egregious, or business in general so bad, that each will, in turn, cut or even eliminate its dividend and your stocks will dip, fall, plummet, or even disappear altogether.

Risk number 2: Long-term interest rates will move substantially higher, and stay there, rendering those fat dividends of yours that much less attractive and depressing the value of all stocks and long-term bonds, not just yours.

Risk number 3: After six to eight weeks of watching your stocks go nowhere except maybe to edge down a little, and of receiving one dividend check for $11 that doesn't quite pay for half a tank of gas, you will become itchy, you will remind yourself that you only live once, you will hear stories about the man over in personnel who turned $2,000 into $17,000 in soybeans in a month—and, feeling bad about having given your broker so little busi-

---

*It is ironic that in the early seventies the bank trust departments, which went so heavily into the low-dividend glamour stocks for their massive pension fund accounts, had nothing to gain for their clients by going after capital gains instead of dividends. Pension funds are not taxed, and so it was particularly inappropriate for the trust department managers to ignore dividends as they did.

ness with this new buy-and-hold strategy of yours, you will call him and ask that he sell you out at a small loss (made no less small by the commissions). Then you will take your money and invest in something fun!

That's the thing. There is a thin line between "investing" and "playing the market"; it is a line that takes great self-discipline to draw; and it is a line that makes all the financial difference in the world.

CHAPTER 6

Choosing (to Ignore)
Your Broker

> What always impresses me is how much better the relaxed, long-term owners of stocks do with their portfolios than the traders do with their switching of inventory. The relaxed investor is usually better informed and more understanding of essential values; he is more patient and less emotional; he pays smaller annual capital gains taxes; he does not incur unnecessary brokerage commissions; and he avoids behaving like Cassius by "thinking too much."
> —Lucien O. Hooper, *Forbes* columnist

Wait a minute (you say). You've told me all this but you haven't told me the part about choosing a brilliant but level-headed, highly experienced, and highly ethical broker. Where's the part about him? If I can find a guy who knows how to make money in the market, and who spends all day at it, why do I have to know about anything but how to retire?

There is a bit in a Woody Allen movie where Woody is standing in line, and a man behind him is lecturing his date, loudly and pretentiously, about Marshall McLuhan. Finally, Woody turns and says (in effect): "I don't know why you're talking so loud, but since you are I have to tell you I think you've got McLuhan all wrong." "Oh, yeah?" says the other man. "Well, I just happen to *teach a course* on McLuhan at Columbia." "Well, that's funny," says Allen, unfazed, "because *I* just happen to have McLuhan right here." Whereupon he goes behind a prop and pulls out Marshall McLuhan. McLuhan looks at the man and says dryly: "You know nothing of my work. How you ever got to teach a course in anything is totally amazing."

Woody Allen looks straight into the camera, at us, and says: "Boy, if life were only like this!"

Indeed. I have terrible news about brokers and money managers generally—news which I expect you've suspected, but couldn't quite believe, all along. There *are* no brokers who can beat the market consistently and by enough of a margin to more than make up for their brokerage fees. Or if there are a few, they are not going to work for peanuts— and any account under $100,000 is peanuts. Or if they will—because they are just starting out in the business or have a soft spot in their heart for you—*there's no way for you to know who they are*. Even if they can prove to you that they have done very well in the past (not just say it—prove it), that doesn't mean they will do very well in the future.

If you get 256 people into a room and give them each a coin to flip, the odds are that half of them—128—will flip heads on the first try. That is the object, you tell them: to flip heads. Of those 128 winners, 64 will flip heads on the next go-round as well. Twice running. Not bad. Thirty-two people will flip heads three times in a row, sixteen people will flip heads four times in a row, eight will flip heads five times in a row, four will succeed six times in a row, two will rack up an incredible seven straight successes, and one—one out of all 256 in the crowd—will flip heads eight times in a row. What talent! What genius!

What nonsense. This man is no more or less likely than anyone else in the room to flip heads the ninth time. His chances are fifty-fifty. He is not a genius, he is a statistic in a probability formula. As is some other man in the crowd of 256 (who may actually *be* a genius) who, odds are, failed eight times running to flip heads.

In any given year, half the stock market players will beat the averages and half will do worse.* After eight years, one player out of every 256—be he broker or

---

* Actually, more than half will do worse because players pay brokerage commissions, stock market averages don't.

mutual fund, private investor or bank trust department—is likely to have done better than average *every single year*. (Except that, since we all want to put our best feat forward, chances are that more than one will *say* he did.)

That player, naturally, will attract quite a following. What talent! What genius!

What nonsense.

I'm not saying the stock market is *all* luck. Nevertheless, it is enough of a crap shoot that luck has a great deal more to do with it than any professional money man is going to want to admit.

By and large you should manage your own money. No one is going to care about it as much as you. And no one but you is going to manage it for free.

This runs very much against the accepted line. The accepted line is that your money is too important to be managed in your spare time: you should let a full-time professional manage it for you even though you will have to pay him to do so.

Who are these professionals and how well do they do and what do they charge? How do you find one who has been right eight times running—and *are* his chances any better than anyone else's to be right the ninth time?

I am being driven from a Boston TV station to Harvard Business School by a fellow alumnus, an investment counselor with an outstanding firm. He is paid not to manage money or to make trades, but, rather, to advise people on how to invest.

His views are not what you would call profound. Before he goes on the air I see him reading another company's views. And those views, in part, would have come from a compilation of other people's views.

In any case, in the car after the show, he is telling me that he doesn't believe "little money," in all candor, *can* beat the averages. He considers $100,000 or less little money. He does think big money can—but he can't say for sure.

"My biggest pitch," he says, "is so simple really—it's that clients shouldn't put all their eggs in one basket. I know that sounds like plain common sense you'd learn in the third grade, it's real simple, but that's what I'm paid to advise." He is paid several tens of thousands of dollars a year; his services are billed out to clients at two or three times that price. He advises Big Money. He recommends utilities on TV *after* they've doubled in price (maybe they'll double again?). Welcome to the world of professional money management.

Item: On June 30, 1967, the publisher, editor-in-chief, and editor of *Forbes* magazine mounted the *New York Times* stock pages on the wall. They threw ten darts apiece, tried again with the darts that missed the pages altogether, and invested a hypothetical $1,000 in each dart-selected stock. Fifteen years later, by 1982, the portfolio had appreciated 239%. Over the same period the Standard & Poor's 500 rose just 35%. And many money managers hadn't done even that well.

Item: Computer Directions Advisors, Inc., a Maryland financial consulting firm, programmed a computer to choose 100 different portfolios of 25 stocks apiece—*at random*—from the 2,700-odd stocks on the New York and American Stock Exchanges. *Eighty-two* of the 100 randomly selected portfolios did better than the S&P 500 over the ten years from 1967 to 1976. Ninety-nine of them beat the S&P 500 in 1976. Concluded *Money* magazine: "These results suggest that it pays to look—as the computer did—beyond the large, intensively analyzed companies in the S&P 500."

Item: On February 28, 1977, the *Wall Street Journal* reported that, "judging by the results of the pooled investment funds banks and insurance companies run, more than three-fourths of the professional managers failed to do as well as the market averages over the past two years. In fact, fewer than one-fourth of them have achieved results as good as or better than the averages, whether for the past year, the past two years or the past four or eight years."

It's not that professional money managers are dumber than average, or lazier than average—just that the market averages don't have to pay brokerage commissions or advisory fees, and so generally outperform people, or institutions, which do.

What is more significant is that among money managers there are exceedingly few who consistently do substantially better than their fellows (or substantially worse). This year's winners may be next year's losers.

In school you can pretty well assume that an A-student this year is likely to do well next year. Not so among money managers. They will flip heads a few years in a row . . . but they are just about as likely to flip tails the next. On Wall Street, it is not enough to be smart and hard-working. There are a great many smart, hard-working people on Wall Street. Smart is taken for granted. Lucky is the way to get rich. (The other way is to be a broker.) Inside information doesn't hurt, either.

As for the not-inconsiderable number of dumb people on Wall Street (and in "Wall Street" I include the entire network of electronic tributaries flowing from all over the world into the mighty Manhattan delta), their existence is undeniable. Which naturally gives rise to the question, If They're So Dumb, How Come They're Still in Business? But this just proves my point: Investment success has at least as much to do with luck, patience, psychological balance (unconflicted greed, for example, versus unrelenting guilt and masochism), and inside information (you don't have to be a genius to be well-connected) as it does with intelligence.

In fact, recognizing the virtual futility of trying to beat the averages, quite a few money managers have gone so far as to invest in "index funds"—funds that mirror the stock market averages, and which therefore cannot fail to do as well once the initial brokerage fee is paid. Such money managers thereby abdicate any responsibility to search out the best values; and they ignore, by definition, the thousands of publicly traded stocks which are not among the 30 Dow Jones industrials or the Standard & Poor's 500. But they are assured of not doing any worse than "average."

It is a cop-out, but it does speak eloquently to the frustration financial professionals have felt in trying to choose "winning" portfolios . . . and it does emphasize the way in which professional money managers will concentrate their investments among a few hundred major stocks, whether the thousands that remain are good values or not.

If the professionals do no better than darts—and most do not—then how much is it worth to have them manage your money?

The answer is that you are probably best off minimizing your "overhead"—paying as little as possible in brokerage and advisory fees. But before we get to discount brokers, it's worth spending some time discussing a theory that has caused much wringing of hands on Wall Street. It is called *random walk*, and to the extent it is valid it helps to explain why professionals are just as apt to blunder as you or I. That is, after all, an intuitively unpalatable notion.

The random walk theory holds that you cannot predict the price of a stock by looking back at charts that show where it has been ("technical analysis"), or by studying the prospects of the underlying company ("fundamental analysis"). On any given day, a stock—or the market as a whole—is as likely to go up as down.

The reason, according to this theory, is that the stock market is "efficient." As soon as a new bit of information becomes known about a company (or the world), it is reflected almost immediately in the price of the stock (or the market). By the time that bit of information filters down to you or me or much of anyone else, it is already reflected in the price of the stock. It has been "discounted."

True, if you happen to be the daughter of the judge who is presiding over a $900 million antitrust suit brought by a tiny computer firm against IBM, and if no one on Wall Street is taking the suit at all seriously, but your daddy has just told you he's going to surprise the pants off those bastards at IBM and award the full $900 million to the little computer company . . . well, then you could probably profit quite handsomely by buying stock in the little computer company. (You could also get yourself and your daddy into very hot water.) You have inside information.

But, inside information apart (and believe me, if you're hearing it from your broker or the company's sales manager's brother-in-law, it's no longer inside information—everyone and his brother has heard it), the market, according to the random walk theory, efficiently digests all the information available to it.

Thus when a company announces higher earnings, the stock may go up—or it may sit pat or even decline. It depends how those higher earnings compare with what the market was expecting. It's not enough to buy U.S. Steel thinking that, with an upturn in the economy, steel profits will be good. If *you* think that, chances are lots of other people have already thought so, too, and the possibility is already reflected in the price. Only if the gain proves more than expected will the price rise.

So you not only have to know what steel profits will be—you also have to try to figure out how that compares with what other people expect. Which gives you not just one, but two chances to guess wrong. Between 1967 and 1982 IBM profits sextupled and its dividend grew eightfold. Yet a share of IBM in July 1982 was actually worth less than in December 1967. It finally did move to new highs as the 1982 bull market took hold, but fifteen years was a long time to wait.

Choosing a horse, you just have to guess which one will run the fastest. With a stock, you have to guess how well a company will do; whether that will make the stock go up or down; and which way the track itself (the market) is moving. (The advantage in owning a stock is that the race doesn't end. You don't have to sell the stock until you want to . . . you *own* something. If you have chosen a good value, you will receive dividends, share in future growth, and with any luck, ultimately be vindicated.)

The random walk theory naturally is anathema to the men and women whose livelihoods and self-esteem depend on convincing clients they know which way stock prices will go. Many studies have been undertaken to refute it. It is in connection with these studies that computers are made to simulate dart-throwing monkeys. Yet the evidence is that it is exceptionally rare for anyone regularly to beat the averages to any meaningful degree.

Burton Malkiel, a professor at Princeton drafted by President Ford to sit on the three-man Council of Economic Advisers, wrote an excellent stock market guide called *A Random Walk Down Wall Street*. In it he made a tight case for random walk, citing numerous rigorously designed and executed studies. Yet he remained himself "a random walker with a crutch." He argued that random walk theory does not have to be absolutely right or wrong. It is *largely* right. It is *largely* true that you can't outguess the market. And it is particularly difficult to outguess the market by enough to justify the brokerage commissions you will incur by switching in and out.

David Dreman, author of *The New Contrarian Investment Strategy*, writing in *Barron's*, made a good case *against* random walk. He pointed out that stock markets have always been irrational—à la Avon at 60 times earnings— and concluded that a rational man could therefore outdo the herd. "Market history gives cold comfort to the Random Walkers," he writes. " 'Rational' investors in France, back in 1719, valued the Mississippi Company at 80 times all the gold and silver in the country—and, just a few months later, at only a pittance."

It is true, I think, that by keeping one's head and sticking to value, one may do better than average. But it's not easy. Because the question is not so much whether the market is rational as whether by being rational we can beat it. Had Dreman been alive in 1719, he might very reasonably have concluded that the Mississippi Company was absurdly overpriced at, say, three times all the gold and silver in France. And he might have shorted some. At six times all the gold and silver in France he might have shorted more. At twenty times all the gold and silver in France he might have been ever-so-rational—and thoroughly ruined. It would have been cold comfort to hear through the bars of debtors' prison that, some months later, rationality had at last prevailed. A driveling imbecile, on the other hand, caught up in the crowd's madness, might have ridden the stock from three times to eighty times all the gold and silver in France, and, quite irrationally, struck it rich.

There *are* rare individuals who can consistently outperform the market. One is the formerly pony-tailed president of the Unicorn Group, a money management firm, Walter Peters. In each of the years from 1968 through 1982, the funds under his management have performed better than 95% of the 3,500 pools of money monitored by A. G. Becker & Co.

Peters relies on an international network of 27 outstanding specialists in politics, economics, and finance—not to pick stocks, but to discern crucial world trends. He is a modern-day Rothschild with 18 "sons" (most of them older than he is) feeding him information.

There is no guarantee that Peters will continue to outperform most money managers, but if you have $1 million, his minimum account, you might give him a call.

Another man who could have made you rich is John Marks Templeton, a fervently but eclectically religious former Rhodes scholar who has managed to beat the Dow by an average of 8% a year since the thirties. Unfortunately, he cannot live forever. A dollar invested in the Templeton Growth Fund at the end of 1954 is worth around $40 today. "Because John felt that God was with him," one associate asserts, "he invested with incredible boldness.

The results make me think maybe he's right—maybe God is with him." Even more instrumental in his success than the Lord, however, may have been his relentless insistence on value, wherever he had to go to find it. He bought European stocks after World War II, convinced that the Marshall Plan would cause business abroad to boom. At one time fully three-fourths of his fund was invested in Japanese stocks, because stocks there were selling at much lower price/earnings ratios than stocks in the United States. When those p/e's rose dramatically, Templeton shifted his equally dramatic profits to countries offering better values.

Templeton shuns growth stocks selling for twenty times earnings and finds smaller, unrecognized companies—in some cases growing equally fast—selling at four or eight times earnings.

It takes special initiative to do what no one else is doing. More than that, it's *lonely*. That, I suspect, is where God fits in.

Successes like Walter Peters and John Marks Templeton poke big holes in the random walk theory, however valid it may be for most investors buying and selling widely followed stocks.

Unfortunately, choosing a winning investment advisor, even if you can afford his services,* is not much easier than choosing a winning stock.

Choosing a winner *broker* will be even harder. Unlike an investment advisor, a broker spends much of his time on the phone selling to new clients, selling to old clients, giving stock quotes and up-to-the-moment market appraisals, talking sports, talking politics, making excuses for recommendations that have gone sour—or handling paperwork, seeing that trades get made, and straightening out back-office snafus. He has little time to search out exceptional values or to formulate broad economic and financial views,

---

* Generally ¾ to 1% of the total assets under management. This fee, unlike brokerage commissions (which you will still have to pay), is tax-deductible. Most good investment counselors will not take on accounts of less than $100,000—it's not worth their time.

as investment advisors and money managers theoretically do.

And unlike an investment advisor, who takes a set annual fee for his services, a broker only makes money when you trade in or out of a stock. Eager as a broker may be to see your account prosper, that is not his first interest. With rare exceptions (and all brokers will claim to be that rare exception), his first interest is to do well himself. His first interest is commissions to feed his family. His first interest is hitting the bonus level at the end of the month that will pay for his family's trip to Disney World. He is as anxious as any automobile salesman that you be pleased with the car you buy—more so, because the better you do, the more business you are likely to give him in the future—but his first interest is to sell you the car. He will never tell you this, but you should never forget it.

Which reminds me:

17. Never buy anything from a broker who calls you up cold. This is so basic as not to warrant elaboration.

If most brokers are wrong as often as they are right—and they are—if the market is *largely* a random walk and if the *Stock Guide, Forbes,* and the *Wall Street Journal* are likely to do as well for you as a team of personal advisors—at a tiny fraction of the price—then why do you need a broker at all?

You need him to execute your trades, to give you stock quotes, to allow you to buy stocks on margin, to hold your certificates, to mail you your dividend checks and monthly statements and annual reports—*and all these services are available from "discount brokers" at discounts ranging up to 75%.* What they will not do is hold your hand, give you bad advice (or good), or, most important, try to sell you anything.

A discount broker won't call you in the middle of the day—in the middle of a root canal, if you are a dentist—to tell you the bad news that's just come over the tape about one of your stocks.

But that's good.

Had he called, you might have panicked into selling. In so many cases, seemingly dreadful news turns out to be news everyone expected, or news about a Brazilian subsidiary that accounts for 3% of the company's sales, or news that pales beside the good news that will be announced the following week. If it's *really* important news, and no one expected it, the stock will be shut down from trading before you can sell, anyway; and when it reopens, sharply lower, the new price will reflect investors' assessment of the news.

With a discount broker, you won't rush into making unnecessary trades. You can finish the root canal in peace.

There is an old joke on Wall Street. "Well," the joke goes, "the broker made money and the firm made money— and two out of three ain't bad." I have heard this joke, often, from a broker with an unobstructed view of the Statue of Liberty and a number of important institutional accounts. One of these accounts entrusted his firm with $175,000 for a flier in options. The institution was shrewd in its timing, as it turned out. The stock market rallied dramatically. Never could one have made as much in options as then. Yet in two months, through an elaborate series of computer-assisted ins, outs, and straddles, the firm's options trader managed to turn that $175,000 into $10,000—generating $87,000 in commissions along the way.

Anyway, if you are already "in the market," making occasional trades, my first suggestion—if you can bear to do it—is that you go through last year's confirmation slips to see what you paid in commissions. You may be surprised. I didn't know I churned my own account, either. Next to rent, it turned out that brokerage commissions were my biggest expense in life.

Adding up one's commissions is a calculation rarely performed. Computerized monthly brokerage statements leave the figure tactfully untallied. For tax purposes, the commission is just lumped in as part of the cost of purchasing a stock, or lumped out as a diminution of the receipts from selling one. (It wouldn't be so bad if the IRS would let us treat the things as the deductible business expenses they clearly are.)

If it turns out you didn't spend much on brokerage commissions last year, fine. But if you are unpleasantly surprised, as I was, I have another suggestion. Not a silly suggestion like "stop churning your account"—a practical suggestion that allows you to enjoy your little vice for less. Switch your account to a discount broker.

Depending on your relationship with your current broker, this may be easier said than done. My own full-price broker is probably the best in his mid-Manhattan office. The brightest, the most personable, the busiest. Our typical phone conversation goes like this:

VOICE: Mr.———'s office.

(Already this is ridiculous because he has neither an office nor a secretary, so this just means both his hands have phones in them and he can't pick up a third.)

ME (*playing along*): Is Mr. ——— in?

VOICE: One moment, please.

HIM: Hello?

ME: Who was that who answered the ph—

HIM: Can you hold on a minute?

(All I want to know is one stock quote, but I want to know it badly enough to hold on.)

HIM: Hi.

ME: Hi. How am I doing?

HIM: Fine, thanks, how are *you*?

ME: Fine. How's my stock?

HIM: Not very . . . can you hold on a minute?

(*Silence*)

(I should really just wait for the evening paper, but because stock quotes are free and an easy way to avoid concentrating on what I'm supposed to be concentrating on, I hold on.)

HIM: Can you believe that guy? He's short 500 Xerox and . . .

Eventually I get my quote, but it takes some doing. Getting a whole list of quotes can be like sitting through a soap opera waiting for the plot tidbits. To keep me listening, once in a while he throws me a quote.

The problem is, we've become friends. Because we're friends I resent it if he's busy when I call. And because I work for a living, I resent it if I'm busy when *he* calls. What's ludicrous is that, because we're friends, he resents it if *I'm* busy when *he* calls. (I installed a special phone, just for him, with a bell I could turn off when I didn't want to be interrupted; but he soon caught on and started calling on the other line, which I had to keep open for business calls.)

So it boils down to this: I wouldn't drop my broker any more than I'd drop any other good friend. And this costs me a small fortune. Three such friends and I'd be out on the street.

I'm paying him to listen to my troubles, and I am paying to listen to his troubles. The fact is, I think my troubles are more interesting than his, and I think my investment advice is as good—so why isn't he paying me? We have often discussed that very point, and he couldn't agree with me more, and I keep paying him (although I now deal with a discount broker as well).

18. Minimize your transaction costs. Unless yours has consistently outperformed the market, in which case you won't believe any of this anyway, you should shop around for the cheapest broker. You will save hundreds or thousands of dollars in commissions and lose little or nothing.

Many of the discounters have branch offices around the country and toll-free numbers you can call if you are out-of-state. (See pages 173–74.) I repeat: Most perform all the services of a regular broker, minus the advice and the chitchat. Full-rate brokers will claim that they provide better executions on trades—that they get you better prices than discount brokers can. However, there is no evidence that this is true, and, on small trades particularly, it is most unlikely.

The only real drawback is the $35 minimum commission most charge. If you are a really small investor, buying $1,000 worth of stock at a time, or even less, that's what you will pay, coming and going—and that's no discount. (Most regular brokers have similar minimums, so it's no premium either.)

So Why Not Hire a Monkey?

Does all this mean a monkey could handle your financial planning? No. It takes intelligence to match your financial strategy with your circumstances: how much risk you can afford, what time horizons you are looking at, what tax bracket you are in. It takes intelligence to try to perceive value. A monkey might buy municipal bonds for a Keogh Plan—but that's like throwing money out the window. A monkey might buy growth stocks for an 80-year-old widow who needs a secure income. A monkey might buy Avon instead of Gulf + Western as the Morgan Guaranty Trust Company, and others, did.

A monkey does not have what investing well really takes: common sense.

CHAPTER 7

Hot Tips, Inside Information—— and Other Fine Points

> If you bet on a horse, that's gambling. If you bet you can
> make three spades, that's entertainment. If you bet cotton
> will go up three points, that's business. See the difference?
> —Blackie Sherrode (as quoted
> by James Dines in *Technical Analysis*)

Hot Tips

Here is what to do with hot tips. If you get a hot tip, make a note of it and pretend to be very interested. But don't buy. If the thing takes off, listen a little more closely the next time this fellow has a tip. If it gets mauled, look bitter the next time you see him. He will assume that you bought the stock; he will feel guilty; and he will buy you a very nice lunch.

Annual Reports

Annual reports are organized very simply. The good news is contained up front in the president's message and ensuing text; the bad news is contained in the footnotes to the financial statement.

You should be aware that for big, widely followed companies, everything of any substance contained in the annual report was known to sophisticated investors months earlier.

Inside Information

It's much easier (although illegal) to make money in the market with inside information than with annual reports.

A Republican I know in the executive suite at a major

insurance company called a close friend of his in a distant city (a Democrat) and told him to buy all he could of a company then selling at $6 a share. Several days later, the insurance giant tendered for the company at $10 a share. The Republican and the Democrat quietly split the profit. A lot of money is made this way on Wall Street, hard though the SEC tries to prevent it.

Or say you are a trader with a major firm and you get a call from one of the big banks asking you to buy 250,000 shares of Digital Equipment. That is a lot of stock. It will in all likelihood move the price of Digital Equipment up a point or two, at least temporarily. You have this friend somewhere you owe a favor and, when you bump into him, you mention that Digital sure looks good for a quick move. He buys options on the stock and makes 30% on his money in two days. Now he owes you a favor.

Unfortunately, very few investors are anywhere near close enough to the center of financial power ever to be tempted by genuine inside information.

Charts

Charts look like they should work, but they don't. Everybody uses them anyway, just as everyone consults astrology columns in newspapers. Some people even take them seriously. Much good may it do them. The various precepts, strategies, systems, rules of thumb, and general folklore that chart readers espouse have been rigorously tested. To quote Malkiel: "The results reveal conclusively that past movements in stock prices cannot be used to foretell future movements [any more than past flips of a coin will help determine the next flip]. The stock market has no memory. The central proposition of charting is absolutely false, and investors who follow its precepts [as many do] will accomplish nothing but increasing substantially the brokerage charges they pay. Yes," Malkiel writes, "history does tend to repeat itself in the stock market, but in an infinitely surprising variety of ways that confound any attempts to profit from a knowledge of past price patterns."

Nonetheless, chartists are likely to be right about as often as they are wrong, and so constantly find new reason to believe in their craft. Their bookshelves bulge.

Don't waste your time.

Splits

Splits are accorded great excitement on Wall Street. Before the split you had just 200 shares of the stock, at $40 each ($8,000), and now—presto—you have *400* shares of the stock, at $20 each (still $8,000). Nothing has happened; your share of the pie is exactly what it was. They have changed your dollars for twice as many half-dollars or four times as many quarters or ten times as many dimes.

The advantages corporations hope to gain from splits are: to lower the price of the stock so more people can afford to buy it in round lots; to make it look "cheaper"; to increase the number of shares outstanding, and hence the trading volume and liquidity of the stock.

While splits can affect a stock's price, at least temporarily, they in no way change a stock's underlying value (or lack thereof).

Stock Dividends

The only difference between a stock dividend and a stock split is that, being a very small split, it is hoped no prospective buyers will even notice that it has taken place.

Stock dividends are under no circumstances to be confused with real dividends. Their (dubious) value is entirely psychological—it is hard to believe that it merits the cost of issuing all those extra little stock certificates and answering the questions of confused shareholders.

Prior to the dividend, 100% of the company was divided among the shareholders. Then, in an attempt to keep those shareholders happy without having to pay them anything, each one is given 5% more shares. Now they have exactly what they had before—100% of the company. It is just divided into smaller pieces.

You pay no tax on a stock dividend, because it adds no value to your holdings. What you hope, however, is that Wall Street will not notice that your company has made this quiet little ''split'' and, accordingly, will keep paying what it used to pay for each now-slightly-less-valuable share.

Sometimes it actually works.

Dividend Reinvestment Plans

These are not the same as stock dividends. Many big companies give their shareholders the choice of receiving their (real) dividends either in cash or in stock. Either way you have to declare the full amount as income. But if you choose to take stock instead of cash, the company takes your dividend, along with a lot of others, and either goes into the market and buys its own stock for you with your money or else sells it direct to you from the corporate treasury.

The advantage to you is that you are forced to save money you might otherwise have spent—if you consider that an advantage—and you pay no brokerage commission to buy the stock. Often, you even get a 5% discount.

The advantage to the company is that it helps keep the stock up (if purchased in the open market), and is a means of raising new capital without having to pay underwriting fees and going through lengthy SEC prospectus procedures (if sold from the corporate treasury).

Although there is no harm in taking dividends in stock, it makes more sense for substantial investors to take the cash and then decide the optimum place to put it.

Utility Reinvestment Plans

There is an added attraction to the dividend reinvestment plans of many electrical utilities. Up to $750 per year of such dividends, if you are single, or $1,500 if you file jointly, may be deferred from taxes until you sell the stock. At that point, if you've held your stock dividends for more than a year, they are taxed as long-term capital gains (otherwise, as ordinary income).

Neat!

The only problems are (1) under the current law only dividends received through the end of 1985 qualify for this treatment, although that might be extended; (2) favorable tax treatment of dividends will be little solace if, in the meantime, the stocks themselves collapse (i.e., you've got to think utilities are attractively priced apart from this added benefit); (3) some utility dividends do not qualify for this treatment (those reinvestment plans where stock is purchased on the open market, and those where the dividends, classified as returns of capital, are already excluded from taxation). Check with your broker or the corporate treasurers of the utilities you're interested in.

Selling Short

When you sell a stock you don't own, you are "selling short." You do this if you think a stock is likely to go down and you wish to profit from its misfortune. To sell a stock short you instruct your broker to (*a*) "borrow" it from someone who does own it; (*b*) sell it; and then, eventually, (*c*) buy it back—hopefully at a lower price than you sold it for—so that you can (*d*) return it. Buying it back to return it is called "covering" your short position.

Selling short is not un-American, as some people seem to feel; neither is it dramatically more risky than "going long" (buying stock outright). True, a stock you buy can go down only to zero, while a stock you short can go up and up and up forever—but few stocks do.

There are three problems with selling short. First, a relatively small one, is that instead of *receiving* dividends while you sit with your position, you may actually have to *pay* dividends. (You borrowed the stock from some nameless, faceless person who does not even know it's been lent; then you sold the stock; now the company pays a 40-cent-a-share dividend, which the lender naturally expects to receive. Your broker deducts that amount from your account and deposits it in his. Silver lining: any dividends you pay out lower your taxable income.)

Second, by selling short you are in effect betting against the management of a company, who are, doubtless, applying their best efforts to making things turn out all right. They could succeed. (Actually, you are betting that *other investors* have not fully grasped how feeble management's competence really is, or what a mess the company is really in, or how little value and potential really underlies its inflated stock.)

Third and most serious, shorting stocks makes the amateur investor even more nervous than buying them. It is not at all atypical for the small investor to spot a stock that is genuinely worth shorting, short it, begin to go crazy as it climbs yet another 20 points, lose his resolve, and bail out at the top—just days before the bottom falls out.

This can even happen to big investors. One man of my acquaintance observed the wild rise in gambling stocks occasioned by the development of Atlantic City and shorted Resorts International, wildest of the bunch. He shorted a lot. And it went up a lot. But this gentleman is nothing if not confident in his acumen, and so he left the country for a six-month round-the-world jaunt, short many thousands of shares of Resorts International, and checked in with his brokers every so often by telephone. Each time he checked in, from country after country, Resorts was higher. The bubble, against all reason, refused to burst. It is easy to say with hindsight that had he held on for just a few countries more the bubble would indeed have burst (all bubbles do), and that all his paper losses would soon have been erased. But there in the Australian outback (or wherever) it had begun to look to my friend as though he might actually lose everything. Discretion being the better part of valor, he decided to cut his losses—$19 million—and cover his short position. That was, of course, the top.

It was a rare mistake for this remarkably successful investor, but a useful tale for the rest of us.

If you do want to short a stock, never short it "at the

market." When you buy or sell "at the market," you are instructing your broker to pay whatever he has to, or accept whatever he has to, to make the trade. The alternative to "market orders" are "limit orders." "Buy 100 shares at 38¼ or better," you tell your broker, meaning that 38¼ is the absolute top you will pay. (You can place limit orders for the "day only," which means that if the broker is unable to make the trade by the end of the day he'll stop trying; or "good-till-canceled," which means you'd better remember to cancel it if you change your mind.)

It is dangerous to short a stock "at the market" because there is a rule about short sales: you may only short stock on an "uptick"—that is, when the price is higher than the "last different price at which it traded." If the stock is falling apart fast, it can be some time before there is an uptick. You wanted to short it at 29½, but placed a "market order"; it trades at 29¼, 29¼, 29⅛, 28⅞, then a block at 28½, more at 28⅛, a big block at 27⅜, more at 27¼, 27⅛, 26⅞, 100,000 shares at 26, and then, finally, somebody bumps it up to 26⅛—an uptick— and that is where your broker calls to tell you that you shorted the stock. (Had you simply been selling it rather than shorting it, you would have made the sale at around 29¼.)

Place a limit on all short sales. Instruct your broker to sell at some figure—say 29, *"or better"*—so that you don't wind up making a trade you wish you hadn't.

Special Offerings

From time to time you may be called upon by your broker to benefit from a "special offering," also known as a "spot secondary." Special offerings are one of the few times where you should consider selling short. Simply put, the special offering is a way of unloading onto the public stock that none of the big professional money managers wants to touch. This is done *not* by giving the public a good break on the price of the stock, in the great tradition of the white elephant sale, but rather by giving the retail broker a fat incentive to push the stuff on his clients—in the great tradition of the hype.

When the broker calls to sell you National Hypothetical—fine company though it may be—don't buy, *sell*. He will stress that you will incur no brokerage fee if you buy the stock—the seller has generously agreed to pick up the tab—but short it anyway. If the stock hasn't fallen nicely within a week or two, cover the short and call it a day. But in most cases, the stock does fall. Cover your short and pocket a quick profit.

Here is an example of a true-life special offering: Sixty-seven thousand shares of Witco Chemical. Witco, a sound prosperous company, had been selling around 32 up until a few days before the offering; the stock was being offered at 30 (of which the seller would receive only about 28½, the rest going to the brokerage house and the broker).

With a special offering there is no prospectus, no advance warning so investors can study the situation carefully—it's hit-and-run, done overnight and into the next day. The stock continues to trade on the floor of the New York Stock Exchange while brokers are trying to unload their special block off the Exchange.

Witco was actually selling at around 29½ on the open market, a couple of hundred shares at a time, while the brokerage firm was pushing 67,000 shares onto its clients at 30. I managed to short 300 shares at 29⅜. Within a day or two it was 28¾. Then quarterly earnings were announced: $1.09, versus $1.22 for the year-earlier quarter. (Is it possible the sellers of 67,000 shares had an inkling?) Two days later the stock was 26¼ (I covered at 26¾). In the fullness of time, the stock might perform well (5½ years later, in 1983, it was up 37%), but the clients who had bought the week before at 30—"Have I got a deal for you!"—couldn't have been too pleased.

One reason stocks go down after special offerings is that the people in such a hurry to sell sometimes have a reason. The other is that such a big sale sops up a lot of demand for a stock, leaving a preponderance of potential sellers and a dearth of potential buyers.

I devote so much space to special offerings not because they occur very often—they've become quite rare—but as an example of what reputable brokers will do, if necessary, to earn commissions. All 67,000 shares of Witco were sold at 30.

The Counter

If there is really a counter somewhere, I have never seen it. "Over-the-counter" is an arena of stocks too small to be (or just not interested in being) traded on a stock exchange. Instead of there being an "auction" market for these stocks, where buyers and sellers meet to do business, there are dealers who keep them in inventory. You want some, we got some.

The problem with O-T-C stocks, particularly if you're not planning to buy and hold for the long haul, is that in addition to brokerage commissions you have the "dealer spread" to contend with. The dealer spread, in percentage terms, can be enormous. A stock may be quoted at 4½ bid, 5½ asked. That means you have to pay the dealer $550 for 100 shares, plus a commission to your broker; and then you can turn around and sell him the same 100 shares for $450, *minus* a commission for the broker. Although that is about as extreme as the spreads get, and although your broker can often do a little better for you than the listed quote, it is still very discouraging. In this example the stock has to rise from 4½ bid to about 6 bid—a 33% gain—just for you to break even.

While you should not rule out O-T-C issues, you must take these often enormous "transaction costs" fully into account before investing.

Portfolio

You have heard of a pride of lions, a medley of ducks, a bevy of quail? So, too, a portfolio of stocks and bonds.

Beta

Beta is a measure of a stock's volatility. When the market goes up, does this stock tend to go up faster? Or not as fast? When the market is falling, does this stock plunge? Or does it just drift downward? The more speculative the stock (or portfolio), the higher its beta. If it moves twice as wildly as the market—a 10% decline in the market produces a 20% decline in the stock—its beta is 2. If it moves only half as forcefully—a 10% market gain produces only a 5% gain in the stock—then its beta is 0.5. Most stocks move about like the market, so, give or take a little, most stocks have betas around 1.

It doesn't take calculus to know that utilities are relatively stodgy and that hot technology stocks are more speculative. But beta quantifies it. "What's your portfolio's beta?" you can ask showoff friends to put them in their places. On the off-chance they have any idea, you should react this way:

> If beta is under 1: "Playing it safe this year, eh?" (Particularly biting if the market has recently been zooming.)
>
> If over 1: "Looking for a good run in the market, are you?"

Beta late than never.
You beta believe it.

The Dow Jones Industrial Average

Against all reason, this highly unscientific average of 30 stocks is the most widely followed "financial barometer"— and probably always will be, which is why, reluctantly, I have referred to it throughout this book. (To see where it's been lately, in broad strokes, see the graph at right. It shows, as well, how the Dow has fared *adjusted for inflation*.)

The Dow is a conservative index. When the market goes

The Only Other Graph in This Book

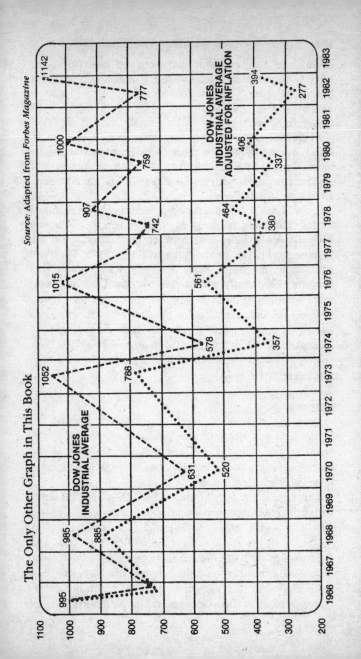

Source: Adapted from *Forbes Magazine*

down, it tends to go down less; when the market goes up, it tends to go up less. Relative to the market as a whole, it has a low "beta."

Other Indices

There are many other indices to look at if you are so inclined, such as the New York Stock Exchange composite index. Possibly the easiest way to compare the progress of smaller companies with the Dow is to follow the American Exchange (Amex) index.

In 1974 and 1975, the Amex index was almost identical to the Dow, only 10 times as small. When the Dow was 830, the Amex index was between 80 and 85; when the Dow was 911, the Amex index might be 91 or 92. Why not "split" the Amex index 1 for 10, I suggested? This would make it easily comparable with the Dow and draw more attention to the Amex, which the Amex then sorely needed. The index remains unsplit, but I continue to add a zero to it and compare it with the Dow. At this writing, multiplied by 10, it has climbed to around 3800; the Dow is sitting around 1120. Amex stocks are less ignored than they were in 1974–75.

Leverage

Leverage is very boring to write about, because no matter how you attack it, you wind up saying what everyone else says, always, without variation, as sure as the caution on every pack of cigarettes: ". . . but be careful— leverage works both ways."

Leverage is buying a house for $50,000—$10,000 down with a $40,000 mortgage—and selling it the year after for $70,000. That's not a 40% profit ($20,000 on top of $50,000)—it's a 200% profit ($20,000 on $10,000). The difference is leverage. You make a profit not just on your own money, but also on all the money you borrowed.

Leverage can obviously improve your return on investment. But be careful—leverage works both ways. If you had to sell the house for $40,000—20% less than you paid for it—you'd have just enough to pay back the bank, but not a penny of your own cash left. You would have lost not 20% on the transaction, but 100%.

Margin

Margin is how brokerage firms make it easy for you to overextend yourself with leverage. They do this by lending you the money to buy more stock than you otherwise could. It's not unlike the credit card a department store will gladly issue, only more profitable for the issuer. On small sums the brokerage house will typically charge you 2% more than the banks charge them. Since they hold your stock in their computer as security, they take no risk. If your securities decline in value anywhere near enough to jeopardize the loan, you either ante up more security, or else your position is sold out, like it or not, before it can deteriorate any further. (Of course, it is just when others are having their positions sold out from under them at distress prices that you should be in there with a wheelbarrow, buying.)

Margin Calls

A margin call is what alerts you to the fact that your life is going to hell and that you *never* should have gotten into the market when you did, let alone on margin.

Options

One way to get incredible leverage is with options.

As if the stock market weren't already enough like Caesars Palace, someone decided the real action would be in trading not stocks, but options. He was right.

Own a stock and you could wait years before it doubles. Buy an option and it can double overnight.

Own a stock and you own a small portion of a company's assets and earning power. Buy or sell an option, and you are placing a bet—nothing more.

Options, therefore, are a great deal more fun than stocks, more potentially lucrative, and more likely to wipe you out. Brokers love them.

If you know which way a stock is going to go, you can make a fortune with options. *But the stocks on which options are traded are, necessarily, the most widely followed and intensively analyzed ones . . . the ones most likely to conform to the random walk theory of price movement.* The hardest ones to outguess. That being the case, the odds in this game are with your broker.

This doesn't mean that I personally have summoned the willpower to abstain from the options market, or that I would pass up for any sum the opportunity to tell you about the time I bought Merrill Lynch options at ⅜.

There I was in the Beverly Hills Hotel, in one of the smaller suites (a converted maid's room), charged with writing a story about the litigation over the remake of *King Kong* ("the most exciting original motion picture event of all time"), but thinking, instead, about Merrill Lynch.

It was the first week in January 1976, and the market had suddenly begun to go wild. Volume on the New York Stock Exchange, which had been running at an unspectacular 15 or 18 million shares a day, was suddenly hitting 30 million shares. Party to each trade, I knew, were a buyer, a seller—and a broker.

Merrill Lynch stock was selling for around 16½. For some reason it had not yet reacted to the surge in volume. It seemed to me that if the volume kept up, Merrill Lynch stock would rise. So I bought 10 Merrill Lynch April 20s. Which means I purchased 10 options, at 100 shares an option, to buy Merrill Lynch stock at $20 a share (the "strike price"), any time between then and April.

The right to buy a stock for 20 when it is selling at 16½ is not tremendously valuable, so it cost me just ⅜ of a dollar per share—$37.50 per 100-share option—$375 in all. Plus $76.88 in commissions.

Stock market volume continued to surge.

Merrill Lynch stock began to move up.

My options began to move up with it.

God, it was thrilling!

As the stock passed 20, the "strike price," the option was being traded at 1½. This was the "premium" people were paying for the chance that Merrill Lynch would go still higher before April (possibly much higher), and that the option would thus actually be *worth* something.

The price I had paid for this option was ⅜. Now it had quadrupled—1½.

I sold two of my options for $300—almost as much as I had paid for all 10. I did this because I am a candy ass.

Stock market volume continued to set records. Why this was happening I had no idea.

I sold two more options at 1¾.

Another at 2¹⁄₁₆.

Two more at 3⅛.

Another at 3⅜ (Merrill Lynch stock was now trading around 22½).

Another at 5½—$550 for an option that had cost me $37.50.

And, finally, the last at 6.

Total investment: $375. Time elapsed: one month. Profit after commissions (but before taxes): $2,397.67.

Options have a certain allure.

Indeed, had I held all 10 until the April expiration date, instead of selling on the way up, I could have turned my $375 into $15,000!

(And had I had the presence of mind, I could have repeated this triumph, on a grander scale, in 1982, when average daily volume began to soar to 70 and 80 million shares, and when Merrill Lynch stock ran from 20-odd up to 70 in a matter of months.)

One thing you have to bear in mind, however, is that somewhere there is a person who *sold* me those 10 Merrill Lynch April 20s at ⅜.

I won. He lost. Between the two of us, we generated $500 in brokerage commissions.

Options are what's known as a zero-sum game—for every winner there is an equal and opposite loser—except it's worse than that, because of the brokerage commissions.

Now. The Merrill Lynch options I have been describing are called "calls." They give the purchaser a call on someone else's stock. If you think a stock is going up, you can buy a call on it. If you own a stock and want to earn an extra return from it, you can *sell* a call on it. The option buyer gives a relatively small bird in the hand to the option seller, in return for a long shot at 10 in the bush. It is a redistribution of risk.

If you play the options game as a buyer of calls, you will have some terrific gains, lots of little losses, and lots of brokerage fees. Your broker will stress that you are getting to "control" $16,500 worth of stock (in the case above) for a commission of merely $76.88—peanuts. But the fact remains that of the $375 you actually invested—your bet—a little over 20% is going to the house. And should you wish to cash in your chips, that's another 20%. The commission rate declines sharply with the size of the trade, but it's never insignificant, even with the largest trades.

Calls are bets that a stock will go up. Puts are bets it will go down. You can buy puts, too.

If you buy a put, you are buying the right to *sell* a stock at a specified price. That right becomes valuable if the stock goes down. Say you buy a General Motors April 70 put. You have the right to sell 100 shares of GM to me (put it to me, as it were) at 70 any time up until April. You pay me $250 for this right, and GM is selling at 73. Then camshafts start corroding all over the country and it looks as though GM will have to recall all its cars. The market panics and the stock falls to 51. You buy it at 51 and put it to me at 70. You have made 19 points a share, or $1,900—minus commissions and minus the $250 you paid me for the put.

All you stand to lose when you buy a put is the cost of the put. If you had shorted GM instead, and it had gone to 110, you could have lost a lot more.

We could go on at some length in this vein . . . I have not yet talked of selling puts, just buying them; let alone straddles (buying a put and a call on the same stock at the same time, hoping the stock will make a dramatic move in one direction or another, but not knowing or caring which), spreads (buying an option at one strike price and selling another at a higher or lower strike price), or any of a dozen other arcane strategies one might employ.

Just remember this: it is a zero-sum game and the odds are definitely against you. Anything you do win (and lots of people do) is fully taxed as a short-term capital gain. There are no dividends, lots of commissions. It may be addictive.

Commodities

Again? I thought we'd disposed of commodities in the first chapter.

Well, yes—but there is no end to the persistence of the nation's commodities salesmen. I once wrote a very negative column on commodities for *Esquire*. In the ensuing weeks, six different commodities salesmen from as far off as Arkansas (that one touting coffee) called—not to complain, but to try to sell me commodity futures. (What do they know about coffee in Arkansas?)

To reinforce your resolve, I quote from investment veteran John Train's *The Money Masters* (Harper and Row):

Stanley Kroll spent 13 years as a commodity broker. He had about 1,000 nondiscretionary customers [customers who made their own decisions with or without his advice]. . . . He even wrote a book on commodity trading. Stanley Kroll says that none of his original 1,000 customers made money. Not one. . . . Kroll and the other commodity specialists I've talked to agree that the retail commodity speculator will almost always sooner or later lose his money, as infallibly as if he cranked away day and night at a slot machine.

And yet away they crank.

Financial Futures

No longer are you limited to speculating in commodities or currencies like cotton, soybeans, copper, or Swiss francs. Now you can buy Treasury bond futures, to bet on the direction of interest rates, and stock index futures, to bet on the direction of the Dow Jones industrial average. All of this is loads of fun and, if you know which way interest rates or the market averages are headed, highly profitable. Unfortunately, you don't know which way interest rates or the market averages are heading, and neither do I.

Options on Futures

With futures, you put up a tiny down-payment to control vastly more of something than you could ever afford to pay for in full. The leverage is enormous. A modest swing in the price of sugar or gold can make you rich (no problem there) or wipe you out. It was to get around this wipe-out aspect of futures trading that Wall Street—Chicago, actually—invented *options* on futures. With these, you will almost surely lose all you invest, but you can't lose more. Now isn't that terrific? Your loss is limited to the size of your bet. They even have options on Treasury bond and stock-market-index futures. Come onnnnnn, WILLow!

Tax Shelters

Tax shelters, other than the ones described in chapter 4, are not the sweet deals many people imagine. At best, tax shelters merely postpone taxes—they do not eliminate them. (At *very* best, as with real estate shelters and research-and-development deals, they can transform today's ordinary income into tomorrow's long-term capital gain.)

Moreover, tax shelters frequently go awry. Some are outright frauds; others are well-intentioned ventures that fail (as in the case of an oil well that comes up dry); and still others do not stand up to IRS scrutiny at audit time.

There are, of course, a great many legitimate tax shelter

deals. But apart from the difficulty of telling the good ones, which are rare, from the rotten ones, which abound, there is the problem that the good ones rarely accept participations of less than $25,000 or $50,000, if that. Which may be just as well, because *only individuals in the highest tax bracket (or soon to be in a lower one) should even consider tax shelters*.

The mistake many people make is to shelter income that might have been taxed at, say, 38 or 40% in the current year, only to see it added to their taxable income a year or two later—and to have it taxed, because the tax rate is graduated, at an even higher rate.

There are other pitfalls as well—ask your accountant about the woes of "recapture" and the agonies of "preference items," for starters.

Those who might benefit can find out about prospective shelters from brokerage firms, as well as from lawyers and accountants who deal with wealthy individuals. But before signing on, seek out the best possible tax and legal advice (no small expense in itself). What's more, investors should satisfy themselves that the prospective deal, even *apart* from its purported tax advantages, is an attractive one. Because no matter how you slice it, in the long run it is very hard to come out ahead by losing money.

Far better, countless investors have found, to lose 50 cents on the dollar to the government than to lose—that's right—the whole dollar.

Real Estate

One "tax shelter" that does make sense for the typical family is a home. The higher your tax bracket, the more of the carrying costs Uncle Sam shoulders by virtue of the tax deductions home ownership provides. Meanwhile, paying off the mortgage provides a good method of "forced saving." Your equity builds month by month, albeit very slowly in the early years.

After becoming their own landlords, the step many enterprising investors take is to become landlord to someone else. For high-tax-bracket investors with the business sense and inclination, buying commercial or residential properties can be very rewarding. Here you get to deduct not just taxes and interest but depreciation and operating expenses as well. (Depreciation is the key to real estate tax shelters, because while you are deducting it from your taxes the property may actually be *app*reciating, instead.)

This kind of real estate tax shelter—where you know the area personally, search for your own investment, and are intimately involved in structuring the deal and overseeing the property—is far different from the kind of tax-shelter deal referred to above, where you are one of any number of limited partners who, come tax time, will sign just about anything put in front of them that promises to defer taxes. The hand-tailored approach takes a lot more effort; but, done carefully, is less likely to go wrong.

Real estate, indeed, can be as much a part-time *job*— scouting for properties, arranging their purchase, fixing them up, interviewing tenants, keeping them happy, negotiating the bureaucratic maze, cajoling plumbers in emergencies—as an investment. Some people see only headaches and risks. Others see a chance to be creative, to build sizable equity (and even more sizable bank debt), and to run their own show. If you are one of the latter, there are a great many primers available, not to mention eager real estate brokers who may go so far as to offer to manage your properties for you for a percentage of the rent. For a clear view of all this, see Albert J. Lowry's revised *How You Can Become Financially Independent by Investing in Real Estate.*

I would only add this caution: The easy money in real estate is finished. There is still money to be made, and tax advantages to help you make it, but you will be hard-pressed to find a bank that will provide you with low-cost fixed-rate financing—the leverage that in the sixties and seventies allowed you to turn a small stake into an empire in a matter of years. Sure, you may be able to get low-cost financing from the seller—but so may you have to provide it when it comes your turn to sell. Nothing lasts forever (even, perhaps, inflation), and the big long run in real estate values relative to "financial assets" (stocks and bonds) seems finally to have ended. Lately it's the financial assets that have been catching up.

Strategic Metals

These are metals like chromium, germanium and columbium that no thriving military-industrial complex should be without. It's just not likely to occur to you to speculate in them—which isn't all that easy, incidentally—when nobody's talking or worrying about them. Only when the world is in an uproar and the prices of these metals are going through the roof, as they occasionally do, are you prey to the pitch. And that, of course, is an even worse time than usual to invest in strategic metals.

Tax Timing

It is common advice that you not let tax considerations interfere with investment decisions. Don't wait for a gain to go long-term, in other words, if it is likely to evaporate in the meantime.

Nonetheless, tax considerations are very much part of the game and it is foolish to ignore them entirely if you are in a reasonably high marginal tax bracket.

As of early 1983, you must have held an asset for a year and a day before any profit you realize selling it can qualify as a long-term capital gain. In the simplest terms, which I will complicate momentarily:

Short-term gains	fully taxed
Long-term gains	only 40% taxed
Short-term losses	fully deductible*
Long-term losses	only half deductible*

---

* Whether you itemize deductions or not, but in any case only up to a maximum of $3,000 a year. Any excess may be carried over to future years.

All other things being equal, therefore, one wishes all gains to be long-term and all losses short-term. That way, if it were not for the Spoiler, one could make an after-tax profit just by breaking even. In the 50% bracket, a $3,000 long-term capital gain would leave you with $2,400 after tax (because only 40% of the gain—$1,200—would be subject to tax); while a $3,000 short-term loss would be 50% absorbed by tax savings—costing just $1,500 after tax. Net after-tax profit: $900.

Unfortunately—the Spoiler—this doesn't work if the gain and loss are realized in the same year. The government makes you net one out against the other. The government is very unfair about this, but such is life. (Equally unfair: If you make a big profit, it is fully taxed; but if you suffer a big loss, only $3,000 of it is deductible in any given year. Where is justice?)

So the real trick is not only to try to keep your losses short-term and your gains long-term to the extent that it's practical to do so, but to take them in different years in order to get the full tax benefits of each.

Realized in any given year	Tax consequences
Long-term gains and long-term losses	OK—the tax advantage of the former cancels out the disadvantage of the latter
Short-term gains and short-term losses	OK—they cancel out
Long-term gains and short-term losses	Lousy—the tax advantages are wasted on each other
Short-term gains and long-term losses	Swell—the tax disadvantages of each cancel each other out

Because short-term losses provide more of a tax saving than long-term losses, it may make sense to sell a loser before it becomes, irrevocably, long-term.

The problem is: if the stock represented good value when you bought it, it might well represent even better value now that it is substantially lower in price. So what you might do is sell it to establish the short-term tax loss—and then buy it right back again. The IRS, however, requires that you wait 31 days before reversing a sale—otherwise they call it a "wash" and pretend, for tax purposes, that it never took place.

So, if you calculate that your tax savings will justify the out-and-back-in brokerage commissions, you could sell the stock to establish your loss, then buy it back 31 days later.

Or, if you have this unreasoning terror that the stock will take off during those intervening 31 days, as it could, you can do it the other way around. Buy a second 100 shares, wait 31 days, and then sell the first 100 for the short-term tax loss.

The day you buy a stock, enter a note in your calendar ten months hence to reevaluate it before it goes long-term; and keep a running tally of your long- and short-term gains and losses as you realize them in any taxable year, so you know where you stand at any given time in making these kinds of decisions.

It's impossible to try to figure out in January or February where you are likely to be, taxwise, near the end of the year (unless you have massive tax-loss carryovers from past years); so in the early months of the year you can let the chips fall as they may. But by the latter third of the year, taxes should be at least one of the factors you consider when you are thinking of selling—or holding—stocks. Not an overriding consideration, by any means, but a real one.

To summarize:

1. Try not to waste the tax benefits of short-term losses on long-term gains—and vice versa.
2. Don't take a short-term gain when, by waiting just a little longer, it would turn long-term—unless you have a very good reason. (However, if you have

already realized substantial losses during the year, it doesn't make any difference.)

3. When you are considering selling for a short-term tax loss, consider buying back the same number of shares 31 days later (or earlier). Otherwise, you could get into the habit of buying high and selling low.

Examples:

• You have no other gains or losses and in November you sell at a substantial profit a stock you bought in January. *Dumb!* Had you waited a few more weeks, your gain would have been long-term, taxed only 40% as heavily— and taxed in the following year.

• You have already realized lots of gains and losses during the year, but so far the sum of your short-term gains (+ $2,200) and losses (–$4,300) is a $2,100 short-term loss. The sum of your long-term gains (+ $400) and losses (–$125) is a $275 long-term gain. OK. What's done is done. Now you are nearing the end of the year and you decide to take (cash in) a $1,500 long-term gain. *Dumb!* The potential tax benefit of the long-term gain is wiped out by your short-term losses. Unless you have a strong reason to sell, why not wait a little longer and take the gain next year, when you might not have losses? Taking the gain now just serves to increase your taxes.

• You have a big tax-loss carry-forward from prior years. You also have a long-term gain in a stock that's been going up like crazy, and you'd just as soon not waste its potential tax benefits by having it netted out against the loss. But your stock has just hit the cover of *Time* magazine and it appears to you quite likely that the jig is up: it looks so good, it must be the top. You say to hell with the tax consequences, sell the stock for a handsome gain, and take the wife and kids to the best restaurant in town. *Smart!*

VSP

Sounds like an important brandy, but is actually what you have to remember to tell your broker to identify *which*

50 shares of Halliburton you're selling. You have 200 shares, but they were bought piecemeal at different times. You may have a long-term profit on some of the shares and a short-term profit on the rest—or even a gain on some and a loss on others. If you're selling just 50 shares, it becomes important to know which 50 they are. You say they're the ones that provide you with a short-term loss, but why should the taxman trust you? The way to handle this is to tell your broker to sell 50 Halliburton "versus purchase ten one eighty-two"—namely, the shares you bought October 1, 1982. Your broker, of course, doesn't care in the slightest which 50 shares you are selling, and he is hardly going to go rummaging around for the right stock certificate, in part because no one seems to use stock certificates any more. They use electronic ledger entries. But your confirm will arrive duly noted "VSP 10/1/82," and all will be square between you and the United States of America.

Re-org

I can't imagine you'll run into this. With luck, I'll never run into it again, either. But in the bowels of most brokerage firms dwells a department called "re-org." My conception of "re-org" is that it is made up of plainclothesmen whose extensions at the firm are unlisted.

I know about re-org because I once owned stock that was converted through some exchange offer for bonds. It was not something I paid close attention to (this is why we have brokers, and why brokers have computers), but every month thereafter an entry appeared in my statement showing that I owned four GEICO bonds. After several months, I disposed of two of them. Several months later, I jettisoned the other two. No problem. More months passed. Then out of the blue came a call from my full-service broker. Re-org, he said, had just notified him they were debiting my account for $1,719. They said I had sold four GEICO bonds when in reality I had only owned two.

"Re-org?" I asked. I couldn't really make out what he was saying.

"Re-org," he said.

"Who in the hell is re-org?" I asked.

"Re-org. They're down in the basement or something. I don't know."

"Well, how can they just take money out of my account? Don't I get to argue about it first?" I asked.

"I argued for you," he said. "You lost."

My broker, who as I've explained is by now a close friend, was genuinely upset by re-org's high-handed tactics—but helpless.

"But the four bonds were in my account for more than a year!" I said.

"I know," he said. "Apparently there should only have been two." He recited a litany of conversion ratios and transfers and journal entries that re-org had supplied to substantiate its case. And it seemed clear (in a hazy sort of way) that re-org was right. But a year later?

"You mean, they can make a mistake and confirm it in fourteen monthly statements and then, out of the blue, come and loot my account?" I asked.

"Yes," said my broker, "and they're going to debit you for the interest you were paid on the two extra bonds, plus interest on the proceeds of the second sale. They wanted you to pay the loss they're going to take to buy back the two extra bonds, because they've gone up since you sold them, but I put my foot down."

(You can see my broker has a lot of clout.)

For weeks afterward I would call with outlandish pronouncements, delivered in my most dictatorial tone, in the name of re-org. "This is re-org," I would bellow. "We see here a dividend check that was not credited properly to the Tobias account in the fourth quarter of 1953. You shall credit his account at once—*at once,* do you hear me?—with 27 years' interest *und* penalties."

To date, re-org has not called to correct any year-old errors made accidentally in *their* favor.

The Only Other Investment Guides You Might Want to Read

As I said in chapter 1, even if this is the only investment guide you'll ever need, it is hardly the only one that's any good. To get an idea of how difficult it is to beat the market, and for a very readable tour of the stock market: *A Random Walk Down Wall Street* by Burton Malkiel (Norton, 1973). For a different slant: *The New Contrarian Investment Strategy* by David Dreman (Random House, 1982). The classic of stock selection, the bible of security analysis: *The Intelligent Investor* by Benjamin Graham (Harper & Row); if you really are going to scour balance sheets for stocks selling well beneath their underlying "value," this is the book.

But remember, the more time you spend reading about the stock market, the more you are likely to want to try your hand. Are you sure this is where you want to put your money? Are you sure you want to begin devoting a good portion of your waking, worrying life in pursuit of this hobby? Have you the temperament to succeed? Can you afford to lose? Have you made out well with past sorties into the market?

CHAPTER 8

What to Do If You Inherit a Million Dollars; What to Do Otherwise

> All I want is a room somewhere,
> Far away from the cold night air.
> With one enormous chair—
> Oww wouldn't it be loverly?
> Loverly—loverly.
>
> —*My Fair Lady*

As television viewers of the fifties all know, coming into a million dollars, even if it is tax-free, is not all applause and confetti. In fact, it can cause all kinds of inner demons to surface.

Listen to Gail Sheehy, author of the huge best-seller *Passages*. Did coming into money cause her any problems?

"Yeees!" she cries plaintively. "It makes me sweat a lot more, it makes me embarrassed and guilty—I mean, truly, it's terrible.

"It's much more fun being the aspirant, because once you have gotten there, even if you are just there temporarily (as you must continually remind yourself you are), you're in a position of defending or protecting rather than aspiring or building.

"It's terribly uncomfortable. It's also a problem that is *totally* unsympathetic to anyone who has 5 cents less than you do. Right? I mean, it's hardly one of the Neediest Cases. So there's nobody you can talk to."

When it first became clear that *Passages* had hit the jackpot, Sheehy was chatting with Random House editor Jason Epstein. Said he: "Yes, well. Money. You will find, Gail dear, that it will now be a dull ache in the back of your head. For*ever*."

"It was so ominous," Gail says, "and it was exactly how I felt!"

Sheehy has been rich and Sheehy has been, if not poor, nearly so. "I can't say that I was happiest when I was living in a fourth-floor walkup on East Seventh Street with a one-year-old baby, you know, carting her on one hip and the wash on the other when I came home from work." But neither is she now laughing all the way to the bank.

Many of us, needless to say, would have an easier time than Gail Sheehy "coping" with a fast million or two. Or think we would. Or would love at least the chance to try.

Still, the problem with sudden wealth seems less how to invest it than how to keep it from wrecking your life. You will notice that in movies and novels where the hero actually manages to pull it off—to steal, win, or discover a fortune—they always end the action there. As if to say that the happiness with which they lived ever after goes without saying. When, in fact, the real story is that the screenwriter or novelist knows full well that this is not true, and can't think of a thing to write that wouldn't be anticlimactic.

Sheehy, with great good sense, is trying hard to avoid what she calls "that classic American trap—which is, you suddenly get a windfall and then, instead of living pretty much as you have, only a little better and with a lot more security behind you—with money there to do something amazing every once in a while when it really counts—you suddenly leap up to meet that income level and always bubble up over it, and then are constantly running to keep up with this tremendous overhead you've established." It is the financial equivalent of the Peter Principle—getting yourself in, no matter how much you have, just a little too deep for comfort.

What to do, then, should you have the ill fortune to inherit a million dollars? Or, worse still, two?

1. Consult a good tax attorney. You can afford it. Explore, particularly, whether there are trusts you should set up for your dependents.

2. Put half the money into a diversified portfolio of municipal bonds of varying maturities, all rated A or better.

3. Buy a country place or a bigger house, if you want one—but not so big that the cost of carrying it will in any way strain the flow of fixed income from your bond portfolio.

3a. If you have the inclination and can find a good value, buy a small rental property. It will provide an inflation hedge and a little tax shelter.

4. Put most of the rest into two dozen stocks of the type described in chapter 5. Good values. Or into two or three no-load mutual funds.

5. Put 5% of the money into silver (100-ounce bars and bags of silver coins), keeping most of it in a bank vault and one bag in a very good hiding place at home. This is your rich man's disaster hedge— a reasonable form of insurance, and, at current prices anyway ($10.50 an ounce), possibly a very good investment.*

6. Be sure your will is in order.

7. Now relax and forget the whole thing. Review it, at most, once a year. Make changes only if your tax circumstances change. Reinvest part of the income each year (if possible, enough to keep your hoard even with inflation), and enjoy the rest.

---

*There are those who think the price of silver may one day equal that of gold. One reason for this is that the world actually needs silver; we don't need more gold. In fact, we have tons of it sitting in vaults all over. Gold's value lies in its scarcity (which digging up more of it does very little to enhance). Over the long term, the gap between the price of the two metals— a ratio as I write this of about 40 to 1—may at least narrow. If so, however well or poorly gold does, silver will do better. (It will also be easier, in the event of calamity, to buy a loaf of bread with an old silver dime than with a by-then $6,000 Krugerrand.)

This is not the way to get every last dollar from your inheritance—but isn't not-having-to-try one of the luxuries that having a million should bring?

Unless you want to switch from being whatever you were being to being a financier; unless you enjoy worrying about money and taking risks and paying taxes on profits and stewing over losses; unless you are intrigued by the machinations of the Fed's Open Market Committee and the effects on the financial markets of the latest fiduciary fad—you should simply structure your assets, should you be so fortunate as to have them in such abundance, so as to give you security, peace of mind, and a good eternal income.

Life is not a business, as my father is fond of saying. Why not set yourself up comfortably and stop worrying?

That's what I plan to do when the man from the contest-judging organization calls up to tell me that by placing my YES! token in the "No, I don't wish to purchase any of these magazines but would like to enter the Sweepstakes anyway" slot I have won first prize. (That will be the day.)

Now what to do in the meantime.

Mutual Funds
Far more practical for most investors than trying to go it alone in the stock market—which is at the very least time-consuming, and possibly a good deal worse for the financially suicidal among us—is the no-load mutual fund.

If stocks are appropriate for an investor, and they may not be, as I have stressed repeatedly throughout this book, then no-load mutual funds may be the best way to go about buying them.

Admittedly, for many investors profits are only part of the objective. Much of the reward is the fun—challenge—intrigue—of the game itself. I am an investor, and I am the first to admit it. But that's not called investing, strictly speaking. It's called playing.

"The prudent way is also the easy way," counsels Paul Samuelson, nationally renowned economist, in a column he wrote for *Newsweek*. Someone else does the research, someone else does the worrying, someone else holds your certificates and provides a record of your dividends and capital gains for tax purposes. ". . . What you lose is the daydream of that one big killing. What you gain is sleep."

Mutual funds provide the small investor with wide diversification and lower transaction costs (because commissions on large trades are much lower than on small ones). Most allow periodic investments of as little as $25, which is perfectly suited to a monthly savings plan. Most are also geared to set up Keogh and IRA accounts with a minimum of paper work and expense. Many are part of a "family of funds" and allow you to switch your money from one to another—from their aggressive-growth stock fund to their tax-exempt bond fund, for example—as often as you like without charge. Just pick up the phone.

With mutual funds the risks of the stock market are still there. Many funds declined 60% and more after the speculative binge of the late sixties and/or in 1973–74. But at least you don't have to make all the foolish decisions yourself. You need only decide which funds to invest in, how much, and when. (See chapter 5, Rules 1–3.) In this very real sense, you are still managing your own money.

The first step in choosing among mutual funds is about the only one that is at all clear-cut. There are funds that charge initial sales fees of as much as 8.5%, known as the "load"; and there are others that charge no load. *Choose a no-load fund*. Or *certainly* no fund that charges more than a 2 or 3% load. To do otherwise is to throw money out the window.*

Statistical studies show that no-load funds perform just as well (and as badly) as load funds. This stands to reason, because that enormous load goes not toward superior man-

---

* An 8.5% load is even worse than it sounds. When you send $1,000 to such a fund, you give up $85 in commissions, so that you are really paying $85 to invest $915—fully 9.3%.

agement of the fund, but to the salesmen who sell it. And they have no influence on its performance. Yet figures for 1980 and 1981 show that of all new fund sales, more than half were of load funds. As long as there are people out selling, there will be people in buying. Don't be one of them.

(If you already own shares in a load fund, the load alone is no reason to sell—you've already paid it. But neither is it a reason not to sell. What's lost is lost.)

In choosing a no-load fund, there are several things to consider. Two things to look at, of course, are the management fee and administrative expenses. These annual charges can be as little as .5% or, with a small fund that can't spread its overhead over a great deal of money, as much as 3% or more. You have to have a very good reason to go with a fund that charges much more than 1% a year for its management and administration. (Many funds will advertise their low management fee without mentioning the annual expenses that are charged as well. Be sure to dig for this number in the prospectus—or ask about it.)

What really matters, of course, is not what a fund will charge you, but what it will *earn* for you. Here you can be much less certain.

Tracked over several up and down cycles in the stock market and graded from A to F on the basis of their relative performance, many funds will rank A or B in bull markets—but D or F in bad ones. This is not because the managers are brilliant some years and dunces in others, but rather because these funds have highly volatile (high-"beta") stocks in their portfolios. Other funds, the less volatile ones, are most likely to rank C or D in up markets, as their stocks climb in the "slow lane" relative to others, but B or A in bad markets, when they merely slip while others slide, tumble, and plunge.

You can see, then, how dangerous it is to choose a fund based on its recent past performance, as many people do. They may buy a fund that has performed even better than the bull market—at the very time that the bull market is petering out and the fund is shifting from its A-rating to its F-rating.

If you knew which way the market was headed at any given time, it would be a simple matter of buying the highly volatile funds at the depths of a bear market, just as things were about to turn, and then switching to the conservative funds (or getting out of the market altogether) just as things were peaking.

However, if you do not have this happy facility—and who does?—then what you are looking for is that rare mutual fund that does better than average in both up *and* down markets, as a few do. Several of these I have listed in the appendix "Selected Mutual Funds" (page 175), although it must be stressed that *past performance is no guarantee of future performance*. Who is to say, even, that the money manager most responsible for a fund's success in a given two- or three-year period is even still at his desk? *People* manage money, after all, not "funds"—and people move on to new and better jobs, or retire.

For an overview of virtually all the available funds, their records of performance, size, and thc like, as well as thoughts on how to choose them, I recommend *The No-Load Fund Investor* (Box 283, Hastings-on-Hudson, NY 10706, $24), an extremely useful, informative guide.

A $10,000 investment in 1972 could have grown in 11 years to $42,000 in the Evergreen Fund—or shrunk to $5,200 in the Directors Capital Fund. Not all mutual funds are alike. Even with mutual funds, and particularly if you choose specialized ones (like United Services Gold Shares or the Energy Fund), it would pay to diversify.

One kind of no-load mutual fund that particularly bears consideration is the "closed-end" fund. Such funds originally sold a set number of shares to the public, raising, say, $100 million to invest. Then they closed the doors to new money. Investors who wished to cash in their share of the $100 million would sell their shares just as they would sell any stock, through any broker to any investor interested in acquiring such shares. Presumably, if the fund managers had turned the $100 million into $110 million, each share in the fund would be worth 10% more than it was at the outset. Or so everyone assumed. But things are only worth what people will pay for them, and shares in closed-end funds sank to discounts that ranged from a few percentage points up to 30% and more. (A few funds rose to premiums.) As I write this, for example, you can buy a dollar's worth of the assets of Baker, Fentress for 75 cents. Or a dollar's worth of the assets of Claremont Capital for 84 cents. This won't do you much good if the managers of those funds have picked a dreadful assortment of stocks that all collapse—but it's just about as hard to pick bad stocks as good, so that is unlikely. More likely, you will have a dollar working for you in the stock market even though you only had to pay 75 or 84 cents.

The risk is that the discount, irrational to begin with, could widen still further by the time you went to sell your shares. On the other hand, the discount could narrow—which at least makes more sense, even if it's not necessarily more likely to happen.

Ask a broker for more information on these funds, which he can trade like stocks. The Saturday *New York Times* and the Monday *Wall Street Journal* carry quotations for these "Publicly Traded Funds" in a separate box in the financial section, including the discount at which each sells.

SCENARIOS

What you should do with your money naturally depends on what the future holds.

• Increased inflation. If inflation accelerates sharply, interest rates will rise and bonds will fall. Most stocks will probably fall, too. If you anticipate accelerating inflation, you want to avoid fixed-income securities. The prices of gold and silver and rare comic books will rise.

• Classic depression. It could be triggered by some international financial debacle or an international trade war or an excess of stringency on the part of the Federal

Reserve—who knows. What makes it so touchy is that the economists are not in control, the psychologists are—and they're not in control either. By which I mean simply that economics has at least as much to do with psychology and confidence, with expectations and self-fulfilling prophecies, as with housing starts or M-3.

If you anticipate a classic depression, you want to buy long-term Treasury bonds. In a classic depression, interest rates will fall to near zero, and you will have what everybody wants: something completely safe that yields (as I write this) 10 or 11% a year.

• The conventional wisdom, at least among best-selling financial writers of recent years, is that we will have some of each. The cycle that's becoming so familiar will continue with ever increasing amplitude: Unemployment and recession will get so bad that the fiscal and monetary floodgates will be thrown open to avert depression, bringing on inflation even worse than the last bout. To fight it, the Fed will slam on the brakes—they have to slam harder and harder each time to have any impact—and throw the country into an even greater slump.

Around and around it goes, inflation, recession, inflation, recession, getting worse and worse. The "malarial economy" Howard Ruff and others have dubbed it—alternating chills and fever.

If they're right, then all you need do is buy gold and silver and sapphires (and a shotgun and a place up in the woods) when the inflation is poised to accelerate; watch them zoom as the currency depreciates; and then, as the brakes are about to be applied, switch from those assets into Treasury bonds. And back and forth, getting richer with each cycle. Eventually, the inflation turns to hyper-inflation as all remaining confidence in paper money collapses. At that point, or in the ensuing depression, the people rise up, or a dictator does, and one way or another we find things very different in this country (so don't forget that shotgun and the place in the woods).

But there is another scenario which should not be dismissed out of hand, unaccustomed though we've become to improvement:

• That this decade, if we keep our wits about us, could become what Paul Volcker has called the mirror image of the last one: falling energy prices, falling inflation, falling interest rates, rising productivity, rising real wages, rising employment.

"Today, we are acutely aware of disturbed capital markets, high interest rates, economic slack, and poor productivity," Volcker said in the summer of 1982—*before* the interest rate gridlock was broken, *before* the stock market took off, *before* there were any signs of economic recovery. "But when the economy begins to expand, productivity should rise. That will permit prices to rise more slowly than wages, encouraging further moderation in wage demands." And further disinflation. "As confidence returns to securities markets, prices of bonds and stocks should rise. Lower interest rates will, in turn, support the continuing growth in investment and productivity." Things could gradually get better and better. "With appropriate budgetary and monetary discipline, the process could be sustained for years."

I make no secret of being partial to the optimistic scenario. I think we've laid a technological base that places us, potentially at least, on the brink of unparalleled prosperity. And there are other hopeful signs.

But my view of the future is no more prescient than anyone else's. What I do know is that the future is unknowable and that one should, as a result, diversify. The folks who tell you with reasonable certainty what's going to happen make me nervous.

I visited Herman Kahn once in 1974 not long after OPEC had jacked up the price of oil from $2 to $12 a barrel. Herman Kahn is a huge man, both physically and intellectually. With the aid of a large staff, he sees the future. He is not shy with his opinions, and he told me that within a year or two at the outside the price of oil would be back down to $7 a barrel. Absolutely. Maybe even less.

If the smartest man in the world can be so wrong about one piece of the puzzle (as Anthony Sampson has pointed out, the index of Kahn's *The Year 2000,* published in 1967, did not even include entries for oil, energy, or Saudi Arabia) can anyone hope to assemble the whole thing?

For the prudent investor, there is no substitute for diversification.

From *Barron's* (December 21, 1981):

"SAN DIEGO—The advertisement, seductively promising a high return on a secure investment, exerted a powerful tug on the elderly woman. Retired and living on a fixed pension, she needed more income. So, she took $8,700—her life savings— and invested it in a second-trust deed, a form of second-mortgage common in California.

"The mortgage broker handling the deal was very reassuring. After all, he said, the property securing the loan was no more than 70% encumbered by mortgage liens and, if a problem *did* develop, she could get her money back five days after sending written notice to the broker's office.

"For two months, all went well. The third month, however, no check came. When the same thing happened the following month, the woman requested the return of her money. Eventually, she learned the nightmarish truth: the mortgage broker was bankrupt and, a lawyer she retained discovered, her chance of recovering much was remote."

Likewise, more than 30,000 other Californians in 1981.

Just because someone in authority guarantees something without qualification—as Joe Granville guaranteed that the 1982 market boom was a trap—doesn't mean you should believe it. Anyone who followed Granville's advice to sell stocks short would have been *wiped out.* "My name is Granville," he later shrugged, "not God."

You may have gotten the same mailing I have several times over the last year. "MORE INFLATION OR A DEPRESSION IN THE 80's?" reads the front of the envelope in big red letters. "Will you lose it all because you guessed wrong?" I've never opened the envelope to see what they're selling, because the notion of staking all you have on one or the other scenario makes no sense.

And if we're lucky, there will be a third scenario—prosperity.

SERMONETTE

Whether you choose mutual funds or a direct plunge into the stock market, bonds, or a savings account; whether you shelter your investments through a Keogh Plan or an IRA; and whether you spend now or save to spend later—you will find that, by the prevailing American ethic, anyway, you never have enough.

D. H. Lawrence wrote a wonderful story years ago called "The Rocking-Horse Winner." "Although they lived in style," Lawrence wrote of his fictional family, "they felt always an anxiety in the house. . . . There was always the grinding sense of the shortage of money, though the style was always kept up. . . . And so the house came to be haunted by the unspoken phrase: *There must be more money! There must be more money!* The children could hear it all the time, though nobody said it aloud. They could hear it at Christmas, when the expensive and splendid toys filled the nursery. Behind the shining modern rocking horse, behind the smart doll's house, a voice would start whispering: 'There *must* be more money! There *must* be more money!' "

One of the children began playing the horses. Before long, in league with the gardener, he had managed to turn a few pennies into a small fortune. The child arranged to have it given to his mother, anonymously. "Then something very curious happened. The voices in the house suddenly went mad, like a chorus of frogs on a spring evening." Debts were paid off and new luxuries lavished—"and yet the voices in the house, behind the sprays of mimosa and almond-blossom, and from under the piles of iridescent cushions, simply trilled and screamed in a sort of ecstasy: 'There *must* be more money! Oh-h-h; there *must* be more money. Oh, now, now-w! Now-w-w—there *must* be more money!—more than ever! More than ever!' "

More is never enough. But there may be a way around this for some people, a way to be just as contented and happy if you don't inherit a million dollars as if you do. It is suggested by this passage from *Stone Age Economics* by Marshall Sahlins:

By the common understanding, an affluent society is one in which all the people's material wants are easily satisfied. . . . [But] there are two possible courses to affluence. Wants may be "easily satisfied" either by producing much or desiring little. The familiar conception, the Galbraithean way, makes assumptions peculiarly appropriate to market economies: that man's wants are great, not to say infinite, whereas his means are limited, although improvable: thus, the gap between means and ends can be narrowed by industrial productivity. . . . But there is also a Zen road to affluence, departing from premises somewhat different from our own: that human material wants are finite and few, and technical means unchanging but on the whole adequate. Adopting the Zen strategy, a people can enjoy an unparalleled material plenty—with a low standard of living.

Or as a friend of mine once said: "It's just as easy to live well when you're poor as when you're rich—but when you're poor, it's much cheaper."

This is not to advocate Buddhism, asceticism, spartanism —or, for that matter, poverty. "I been poor and I been rich—and honey, rich is better"—and all that. Naturally. I, for one, like living a little better every year. In fact, I believe happiness lies less in how much you have than in which way you're headed. Which is a strong argument for saving something each year rather than see your net worth slip backward; and for *pacing* your acquisition of the finer things, lest the day come when you can't afford them. For remember: a luxury once sampled becomes a necessity. It's not so bad living on a low floor—until you've had a view.

Ultimately, how you should spend or invest your money depends not so much on price-earnings ratios or dividend rates as on those larger questions that forever lurk, but generally go unasked: Who am I? What am I trying to do with my life? Is money the means or the end?

There is a good measure of self-knowledge required to choose the proper investment course. It has even been postulated that many small investors in the stock market, without knowing it, secretly want to lose. They jump in with high hopes—but feeling vaguely guilty. Guilty over "gambling" with the family's money, guilty over trying to "get something for nothing," or guilty over plunging in without really having done much research or analysis. Then they punish themselves, for these or other sins, by selling out, demoralized, at a loss.

In any event, whether or not they secretly want to, many investors, failing to seek out value and then hold it patiently, do lose. If this little book saved you $1,000 a year—on wine (by the case, on sale), on life insurance and finance charges, on brokerage commissions (trading less often, and with a discount broker), on investment letters (not subscribing to them), and on taxes (particularly with a Keogh Plan or IRA)—I would be delighted. But if it saved you from getting burned in the stock market, or on even one seemingly surefire "investment" someone was trying to sell you—I would be thrilled!

(I hear, by the way, that the Mexican peso is now very strong again, and that you can get a hell of an interest rate south of the border.)

Appendices

Twenty-five Things You Might Not Have Thought of That Could be Tax-Deductible

1. Abortions*

2. Face lifts, hair transplants, and other cosmetic surgery*

3. Travel to and from your psychiatrist*

4. The swimming pool your doctor ordered you to build for the daily regimen you require to avoid paralysis*†

5. Calls to your broker—if you make two each business day, $50 a year

6. Calls (from a pay phone or elsewhere) to your modeling agency, agent, secretary, business-related answering service, accountant, or attorney (if on business or tax matters)

7. The *Wall Street Journal*, delivered or from the newsstand each morning; *Barron's*, *Business Week*, *Forbes*, *Fortune*, trade journals, *Money*

8. Diners Club or American Express annual dues, if you can argue that you would not have needed the extra card if it were not for your business entertaining

---

* Medical expenses, prescription drugs, and health insurance premiums are deductible only to the extent that, in sum, they exceed 5% of your adjusted gross income.
† The amount that may be deducted is the total cost of the pool minus the market value it adds to your home.

9. Postage for business correspondence—to broker, for payment of business bills, etc.

10. Answering service (or machine), if needed for business

11. Full value of securities or other property you give to charity, even if it has appreciated since you bought it, so long as you have held it more than a year (if held less than a year, you get to deduct only your cost)

12. Safe-deposit-box rental (if needed to store securities, tax records, or other business-related material)—and trips to and from

13. Transportation to and from volunteer work, plus expenses

14. Tax-preparation fees

15. Speed-reading course, if directly beneficial to current career; likewise, computer courses

16. Installment interest, margin interest, credit card interest—even interest charged by the government itself on late taxes

17. Pocket calculator if purchased for business or taxes or investments (home computer, likewise)—plus batteries

18. Business gifts if given to improve the chances for future sales (up to $25 per individual per year)

19. Christmas cards sent to clients, patients, or customers— plus postage

20. Capital losses up to $3,000

21. Equipment or furnishings (typewriters, desks, carpet, copiers, answering machines, etc.) used for business

may be depreciated. *They may also qualify for the investment tax credit.* Write local IRS office for the rules and note that up to $5,000 of business equipment (climbing to $7,500 in 1984) may be deducted all at once (expensed) rather than depreciated

22. Video tape recorder, if bought to tape programs you need to see for business but would otherwise have had to miss

23. Passport fee and passport photo cost if you travel for business

24. Attaché case; stopwatch if you're a track coach; watch repair if watch is needed at work

25. Transportation to and from the IRS audit that will almost surely result from your taking deductions such as these

How Much Life Insurance Do You Need?

Probably more than you can afford. However, you can stretch your coverage by purchasing term instead of whole life, and by shopping for it carefully (see pages 22–25).

Naturally, the amount of life insurance you should carry depends on your circumstances. If you are single with no dependents, you need little—to assist with burial expenses or, posthumously, pay off a few debts—or none. The great push to sell college students life insurance is not entirely unlike the selling of ice to Eskimos, except that a lot more insurance is sold that way than ice.

If you are married, with a hopelessly incompetent spouse, a family history of heart disease, and a host of little children, you should carry a great deal of insurance. Less if your spouse has a reliable income. Less still if you have fewer children or if those children have wealthy and benevolent grandparents. And still less once those children have grown up.

If you are very rich, you need no insurance at all, except as it is helpful in paying off estate taxes. If you *live* richly off a high income but own outright little more than a deck of credit cards and some cardigan sweaters, it will take a lot of insurance to keep from exposing your dependents to an altogether seamier side of life when you are gone.

What you want, ideally, is enough insurance, when combined with whatever other assets you may have, to pay for what are euphemistically called "final expenses" (deathbed medical expenses not covered by other insurance, funeral expenses, and possible postmortem emergencies like an illness of the surviving spouse, payment of bills you didn't know had been incurred, auto repair, and so on)—and then enough in addition to replace the income you had been kicking into the family till. So that, financially, anyway, you will not be missed.

For final expenses and a cushion for emergencies figure an amount equal to roughly half one year's gross salary; or, to be on the safe side—particularly if your income is under $15,000—a full year's income.

But that's nothing compared to what you will need to replace your income. (Or, if you are a homemaker, what your spouse will need to hire someone to replace your services.) Of course, you don't have to replace all of it, just the after-tax portion you were actually taking home. And not even that much, because with you gone, there will be one fewer mouth to feed, one fewer theater ticket to buy* . . . Your surviving dependents will need anywhere from 60 to 80% of your current take-home pay in order to live as well, or nearly as well, as they were living before. So if you were earning $30,000 a year and taking home $23,000, your family might maintain roughly the same living standard on $14,000 to $18,500 a year.

A portion of this replacement income will be provided by (tax-free) Social Security benefits. The typical $8,000-16,000 annual benefit a widow with one or more dependent children receives will go a long way toward replacing 60% of the deceased's after-tax income. Thus, low-income families need not rely nearly as much on insurance as higher-income families, so long as they are covered by Social Security.

How much of an "endowment" will it take to make up the gap between Social Security payments and what you actually need? Let's say your take-home pay is $30,000, of which you would like to replace $23,000, and that Social Security would in your case amount to $16,000 (until the children are grown). The gap is $7,000 a year.

If you wanted a large enough "endowment," or "annuity," to pay your surviving spouse $7,000 a year for

---

* Not to mention the savings on commuting expenses, cigarettes, medical and dental expenses, gambling losses, the subscription to *Business Week*, insurance premiums, gifts, charitable contributions, clothing, laundry, golf balls, and toiletries and cosmetics.

20 years, and if we assumed he or she would be able to invest the insurance money to return 6% after taxes, then you would need to carry $80,000 in life insurance. You don't need such a large sum that it will throw off $7,000 a year in interest forever, because your surviving spouse will not live forever. He or she can gradually eat up the principal as well as the interest. To provide a $7,000 annuity that would last *40* years under the same assumptions would require $105,000. However, if you wanted the $7,000 payment to increase with inflation, and assumed that the "real" rate of interest your spouse could earn on this money, after taxes and after netting out inflation, were 3%, you would need $104,000 to provide $7,000-a-year-plus-enough-to-cover-inflation for 20 years, $162,000 for 40 years.

The table that follows shows how much life insurance is needed to provide various levels of after-tax annual income for varying lengths of time. It assumes the insurance proceeds will be invested at a mere 3% after taxes, which may approximate the true return, after inflation, your heirs could hope to earn. By assuming an inflation-adjusted interest rate, you are assuring that each $1,000 a year your heirs receive will be equivalent to $1,000 of today's buying power. Naturally, if you assume they could earn a higher interest rate, the amount of insurance you would need would decline drastically. To make this point, I have included in parentheses figures that assume an 8% after-tax return. The problem is that unless your heirs are extraordinarily clever in investing these proceeds (or reckless-but-lucky), they will only be able to earn such a high rate if inflation, too, is running at a high rate . . . in which case the value of their payment each year will shrink and shrink.

If these figures look overwhelming (and they do), remember that they may be reduced by the value of assets you already own and that the income they will provide sits on top of Social Security benefits. Also, your spouse could remarry; your spouse could go to work; once the children

How much insurance you must carry to provide . . .				
this much annual income . . .		. . . for this many years		
	10 years	**20 years**	**30 years**	**40 years**
$1,000	**$8,500** ($6,700)	**$15,000** ($10,000)	**$20,000** ($11,250)	**$23,000** ($12,000)
$2,500	**$21,000** ($17,000)	**$37,500** ($25,000)	**$50,000** ($27,500)	**$57,500** ($30,000)
$5,000	**$42,500** ($33,500)	**$75,000** ($50,000)	**$100,000** ($55,000)	**$115,000** ($60,000)
$7,500	**$64,000** ($50,000)	**$112,500** ($75,000)	**$150,000** ($85,000)	**$172,000** ($90,000)
$10,000	**$85,000** ($67,000)	**$150,000** ($100,000)	**$200,000** ($112,500)	**$230,000** ($120,000)
$15,000	**$128,000** ($100,000)	**$225,000** ($150,000)	**$300,000** ($170,000)	**$345,000** ($180,000)

NOTE: Main entries assume benefits will earn 3% after inflation and taxes; parenthetical entries—8%.

are grown, they could provide support as well. Furthermore, it is not inconceivable that your family could be happy with a more modest life style than they now enjoy.

Nine Simple Steps to Your Answer

1. Determine how much your family would need annually to live nicely without you ..... _____ (Annual Needs)

2. Subtract from this the approximate annual Social Security benefit your family would receive if you died today (see pages 168–9), and any other income they would continue to receive in your absence .... – _____ (Annual Income)

3. The difference is the annual gap you will want your life insurance to make up .... _____ (Annual Gap)

4. Using the figure in step 3 ("Annual Gap"), consult the table on page 166 to find the approximate "endowment" you would need to close this gap for the desired number of years .. _____ ("Endowment" Required)

5. Add to this a provision for "final expenses" equal to 50 or even 100% of a full year's gross salary .... + _____ (Final Expenses)

6. The total of steps 4 and 5 is the maximum amount of insurance coverage you would need . _____ (Gross Insurance Needed)

7. From this you should subtract the value of other assets you may own, such as savings accounts, stocks and bonds, a pension or profit-sharing plan at work, a group life insurance policy at work (do not include equity in your home, as you will not want your heirs to have to sell it or to increase the mortgage) .... – _____ (Other Assets)

8. Finally, adjust downward for such intangibles as wealthy grandparents, or a spouse who is resourceful, employable, or likely to remarry. If you feel your survivors could manage in a less expensive home, subtract the difference between what they could get for your present one and what the new one would cost .... – _____ (Intangible Adjustments)

9. This is roughly the amount of life insurance you should, if at all possible, be carrying. Review these calculations as your circumstances change .... _____ (Net Life Insurance Needed)

How to Figure Your
Social Security Benefits

There is no way to know exactly what your Social Security benefits will be when you (or yours) begin to collect them. However, you can probably get a pretty good idea by looking to see what they would be *now*, were you to retire, die, or become disabled today.

Social Security benefits are likely to rise with the cost of living. But in *real dollars, real buying power*, it's reasonable to assume that the payments will neither increase (how could we afford it?) nor decrease sharply (how could Congress allow it?). The operative word here would seem to be "sharply," because clearly the squeeze is on. As national demographics tilt ever more heavily toward older Americans, there will be ever fewer workers to support ever greater numbers of retirees. Thus, it is likely the retirement age will gradually be pushed back, and that benefits, expressed as a measure of buying power, have peaked.

Social Security benefits are tied to how much you have paid in to the system. What's more, in the case of death benefits, the payout to your surviving spouse will depend in part on your age at death and on the composition of your family. Therefore, the examples on the next page are to be taken as *only the roughest guideline* of what you might expect.

The figures assume, at the low end, that the worker has averaged about $4,000 in Social Security–taxed earnings a year since 1950; and, at the high end, that the worker has in all years earned at least as much as the top income level on which Social Security tax was levied. As recently as 1965, only the first $4,800 of earnings was subject to Social Security tax. By 1983, that figure had climbed to $35,700.

Examples of Annual *Tax-free* Income from Social Security

Recipient	Amount
Worker retiring at 65, with no dependents	$5,328– 8,748
Worker retiring at 65, with dependents	9,444–15,312
Disabled worker, no dependents	5,328– 9,216
Disabled worker with dependents	5,328–13,824
Widow or widower at 65	5,328– 8,748
Widow or widower caring for one child	7,993–13,824
Widow or widower caring for more than one child	9,444–16,140

To qualify for benefits, no one needs credit for more than ten years of work covered by Social Security. The length of credit required ranges down to as little as 1½ years for people who become disabled or die in their early twenties.

If you are within several years of retirement, don't rely on the rough guidelines above. Write or call any of the 1,300 Social Security offices around the country and ask for the booklet and forms that will help you make a closer estimate.

Cocktail Party Financial Quips
to Help You Feel Smug

1. If you are fully invested in the market (or wish to pretend you are), you can say: "I'm betting that the Fed will ease up." This means you think the Federal Reserve Board will ease up on interest rates, allowing them to fall and the stock market, as a consequence, to rise. Either this is the general consensus, in which case you will seem *au courant;* or else it is a contrary opinion, in which case you will appear to be a shrewd man or woman of independent thought. No matter what "the Fed" is really doing, or how little you know of it or care, that you should have an opinion at all is impressive. If someone tries to pin you down, look genuinely uncomfortable—which won't be hard under the circumstances—and say, just a bit mysteriously: "Forgive me, but I'd rather not discuss it just yet."

2. If you've cautiously avoided the stock market, but someone asks you what you're into these days, you can say: "Gee, Bill, I really don't have much of a mind for stocks. I know I must be missing out on some terrific opportunities, but I'm happier just sticking to municipals." This will be taken as a display of false modesty—it will be assumed you really do have a mind for stocks—and it will indicate that you are a high-bracket taxpayer of considerable means. You will be envied.

3. Or: "I'll tell you the truth, Phil, I used to play the market until I totted up how much time I was spending on it—you know, the calls from my broker, checking the stock pages, juggling the commodity straddles to save a few tax dollars. I decided I'd rather spend the time with my kids and settle for a sure 8 or 10 percent in bonds." This is bound to make Phil feel guilty.

4. If someone is waxing philosophical about the market, you can say: "The great mistake made by the public is paying attention to prices instead of values." If that raises an eyebrow, because it sounds a bit more formal than you usually sound, you can continue: "C. H. Dow said that back at the turn of the century [which he did], and it's as true now as it was then [which it is]."

5. If someone is boasting about a stock that's really zoomed, you can say: "Gosh, that's terrific! Sounds like it's time to short some."

6. Or (if you're really fed up) you could say: "Gee, a regular Hetty Green!" Chances are, your companion will have no notion who Hetty Green, "the witch of Wall Street," was. (She died in 1916 leaving $100 million to children who despised her.) But, if his fists clench, suggesting that he does know who Hetty was, after all, flash a quick grin and say: "Just kidding, Phil. Just kidding."

Sample Brokerage Commissions

The table below shows typical commission rates full-service brokers were charging in 1983. Many were nonetheless giving even small clients modest discounts, when pressed to do so. *Discount* brokers typically beat the rates shown here by 35 to 75%. The hitch: most charged a $30 or $35 minimum. On small trades, little or nothing would be saved.

Commmissions for trades involving less than $10,000

Stock price	100 shares	200 shares	300 shares	500 shares	1,000 shares
$ 1	$25 (50%)	$25 (25%)	$30 (20%)	$50 (20%)	$100 (20%)
$ 5	$30 (12%)	$48 (9.6%)	$71 (9.5%)	$106 (8.5%)	$182 (7.3%)
$10	$37 (7.4%)	$71 (7.1%)	$95 (6.3%)	$138 (5.5%)	$252 (5%)
$15	$46 (6.1%)	$87 (5.8%)	$114 (5.1%)	$174 (4.6%)	
$20	$54 (5.4%)	$99 (5%)	$136 (4.5%)	$204 (4.1%)	
$25	$62 (5%)	$111 (4.4%)	$155 (4.1%)		
$40	$82 (4.1%)	$152 (3.8%)		Involves more than $10,000	
$75	$94 (2.6%)				

NOTE: Figures in parentheses represent the *round-trip* brokerage fee you incur in buying, and eventually selling, the amount of stock indicated.

Selected Discount Brokers

The addresses listed below are the main offices of six of the best discount brokers. All have branch offices in other cities as well, and toll-free numbers for out-of-state customers. Commission schedules vary—find the one that best matches the kind of trading you do. All are insured up to $500,000 per account.Compare services also: Is margin available? At what rates? What discounts are available on options? How long are you kept waiting on "hold" on a busy day? Will the firm hold your securities for you? Send you S&P sheets? Take orders and provide account information after normal business hours? Accept IRA and Keogh accounts? Allow you to write checks against the value of your securities? Reimburse you for the cost of an in-home stock quote service?

Company	Minimum Commission
Charles Schwab & Co. 1 Second St. San Francisco, CA 94105 (800) 648-5300	$18 + 1.2% of value of trade
Fidelity Brokerage 161 Devonshire St. Boston, MA 02110 (800) 225-2097	$30
Rose & Co. Board of Trade Bldg. Chicago, IL 60604 (800) 621-3700	$20 + 5¢/share

Discount Brokerage $35
67 Wall St.
New York, NY 10005
(800) 221-4257

Waterhouse Securities $35
120 Wall St.
New York, NY 10005
(800) 221-8392

York Securities $35
44 Wall St.
New York, NY 10005
(800) 221-3154

Selected Mutual Funds

If you are serious about selecting a mutual fund, send $24 for *The Handbook for No-Load Mutual Funds* (Box 283, Hastings-on-Hudson, NY 10706). It provides exactly the kind of helpful information and advice any prospective mutual fund buyer should have.

The following no-load funds have done reasonably well in up and in down markets. Although this is no guarantee that they will continue to do well, it may be worth your while writing for their prospectuses and latest reports:

Evergreen Fund
550 Mamaroneck Ave.
Harrison, NY 10528
(914) 698-5711

Fidelity Equity Income Fund
82 Devonshire St.
Boston, MA 02109
(800) 225-6190

Guardian Mutual Fund
342 Madison Ave.
New York, NY 10173
(212) 850-8300 (collect)

Mutual Shares Corporation
26 Broadway
New York, NY 10004
(800) 221-7864

20th Century Select
Box 200
Kansas City, MO 64141
(816) 531-5575

Value Line Fund
711 3rd Ave.
New York, NY 10017
(800) 223-0818

The performance of one load fund has been so extraordinary as to warrant inclusion, even though other load funds with excellent records are not listed here. It is the Templeton Growth Fund, 44 Victoria St., Toronto M5C 1Y2, Ont., Canada (800 237-0738). Unfortunately, there is no assurance of how many more years Templeton himself will manage the fund.

A few groups of large no-load funds—not necessarily those with the best performance records—offer the added convenience of "telephone switching," which allows investors to transfer money from one fund to another within the "family" just by calling a toll-free number. Thus, if one felt he could foretell the direction of stock prices or interest rates, he could switch from stocks to bonds to short-term instruments, and back. All this can be done while remaining under the tax shelter of a Keogh Plan or IRA. For more information, call these fund families, toll free:

> Dreyfus: (800) 223-5525
> Fidelity: (800) 225-6190
> Financial: (800) 525-6148
> Rowe Price: (800) 638-1527
> Value Line: (800) 223-0818
> Vanguard: (800) 523-7910

Even if you are wrong in calling stock market moves, you will at least not incur huge brokerage fees as you move in and out of the market.

Fun with Compound Interest

If you have not yet learned how to work the compound-interest key on your pocket calculator, but wish to astound your friends anyway, here is how $1 (or any multiple of $1) would grow at varying rates of interest, compounded annually. Compounded daily it would grow even a little faster. Unfortunately, if you are able to earn a very high rate of interest over a long period of time, it is likely to be because inflation is running at nearly as high a rate. *Net of inflation and taxes, it's no cinch to earn 3 to 4% consistently*, let alone any more. Still, it's fun to think about.

How a Dollar Grows*

Year	3%	5%	6%	7%	8%
1	$1.03	$ 1.05	$ 1.06	$ 1.07	$ 1.08
2	1.06	1.10	1.12	1.14	1.17
3	1.09	1.16	1.19	1.23	1.26
4	1.13	1.22	1.26	1.31	1.36
5	1.16	1.28	1.34	1.40	1.47
6	1.19	1.34	1.42	1.50	1.59
7	1.23	1.41	1.50	1.61	1.71
8	1.27	1.48	1.59	1.72	1.85
9	1.30	1.55	1.69	1.84	2.00
10	1.34	1.63	1.79	1.97	2.16
11	1.38	1.71	1.90	2.10	2.33
12	1.43	1.80	2.01	2.25	2.52
13	1.47	1.89	2.13	2.41	2.72
14	1.51	1.98	2.26	2.58	2.94
15	1.56	2.08	2.40	2.76	3.17
20	1.80	2.65	3.21	3.87	4.66
25	2.09	3.39	4.29	5.43	6.85
30	2.43	4.32	5.74	7.61	10.06
35	2.81	5.52	7.69	10.68	14.79
40	3.26	7.04	10.29	14.98	21.72
50	4.38	11.47	18.42	29.47	46.90
100	$19	$132	$339	$868	$2,200
200	$369	$17,292	$115,125	$753,849	$4.8 million

*To see how $3, or $1,000, or any other figure would grow, simply multiply by 3, or 1,000, or that other figure.

10%	12%	15%	20%	Year
$ 1.10	$ 1.12	$ 1.15	$ 1.20	1
1.21	1.25	1.32	1.44	2
1.33	1.40	1.52	1.73	3
1.46	1.57	1.75	2.07	4
1.61	1.76	2.01	2.49	5
1.77	1.97	2.31	2.99	6
1.95	2.21	2.66	3.58	7
2.14	2.48	3.06	4.30	8
2.36	2.77	3.52	5.16	9
2.59	3.11	4.05	6.19	10
2.85	3.48	4.65	7.43	11
3.14	3.90	5.35	8.91	12
3.45	4.36	6.15	10.70	13
3.80	4.88	7.08	12.84	14
4.18	5.47	8.14	15.41	15
6.72	9.65	16.37	38.34	20
10.83	17.00	32.92	95.40	25
17.45	29.96	66.21	$237	30
28.10	52.80	$133	$591	35
45.26	93.05	$267	$1,469	40
$117	$289	$1,083	$9,100	50
$13,780	$83,523	$1.17 million	$82.8 million	100
$190 million	$7.0 billion	$1.4 trillion	$6.9 quadrillion	200

ABOUT THE AUTHOR

ANDREW TOBIAS is the author of THE FUNNY MONEY GAME; the bestselling biography of Charles Revson, FIRE AND ICE; a collection of stories called GETTING BY ON $100,000 A YEAR (AND OTHER SAD TALES); a bestseller on the insurance industry, THE INVISIBLE BANKERS; and his most recent book is MONEY ANGLES. He is also the author of the bestselling computer software package, MANAGING YOUR MONEY. He is a graduate of Harvard College and Harvard Business School. A former contributor to NEW YORK and ESQUIRE magazines, he now writes a quarterly column for PLAYBOY.